CW00369824

AAT

Qualifications and Credit Framework (QCF)
LEVEL 4 DIPLOMA IN ACCOUNTING

TEXT

Credit Management
and Control

2011 Edition

First edition July 2010

Second edition June 2011

ISBN 9780 7517 9738 1 (Previous edition 9780 7517 8569 2)

British Library Cataloguing-in-Publication Data
A catalogue record for this book is available from the British
Library

Published by

BPP Learning Media Ltd
BPP House
Aldine Place
London
W12 8AA

www.bpp.com/learningmedia

Printed in the United Kingdom

CONTENTS

INTRODUCTION

Since July 2010 the AAT's assessments have fallen within the **Qualifications and Credit Framework** and most papers are now assessed by way of an on demand **computer based assessment**. BPP Learning Media has invested heavily to produce new ground breaking market leading resources. In particular, our **suite of online resources** ensures that you are prepared for online testing by means of an online environment where tasks mimic the style of the AAT's assessment tasks.

The BPP range of resources comprises:

- **Texts**, covering all the knowledge and understanding needed by students, with numerous illustrations of 'how it works', practical examples and tasks for you to use to consolidate your learning. The majority of tasks within the texts have been written in an interactive style that reflects the style of the online tasks the AAT will set. Texts are available in our traditional paper format and, in addition, as ebooks which can be downloaded to your PC or laptop.

- **Question Banks**, including additional learning questions plus the AAT's practice assessment and a number of other full practice assessments. Full answers to all questions and assessments, prepared by BPP Learning Media Ltd, are included. Our question banks are provided free of charge in an online environment which mimics the AAT's testing environment. This enables you to familiarise yourself with the environment in which you will be tested.

- **Passcards**, which are handy pocket-sized revision tools designed to fit in a handbag or briefcase to enable you to revise anywhere at anytime. All major points are covered in the Passcards which have been designed to assist you in consolidating knowledge.

- **Workbooks**, which have been designed to cover the units that are assessed by way of project/case study. The workbooks contain many practical tasks to assist in the learning process and also a sample assessment or project to work through.

- **Lecturers' resources**, providing a further bank of tasks, answers and full practice assessments for classroom use, available separately only to lecturers whose colleges adopt BPP Learning Media material. The practice assessments within the lecturers' resources are available in both paper format and online in e format. What fantastic news: you can now give your students an online mock.

This Text for Credit Management and Control has been written specifically to ensure comprehensive yet concise coverage of the AAT's new learning outcomes and assessment criteria. It is fully up to date as at June 2011 and reflects both the AAT's unit guide and the practice assessment provided by the AAT.

Each chapter contains:

- clear, step by step explanation of the topic

- logical progression and linking from one chapter to the next

- numerous illustrations of 'how it works'

- interactive tasks within the text of the chapter itself, with answers at the back of the book. In general, these tasks have been written in the interactive form that students will see in their real assessments

- test your learning questions of varying complexity, again with answers supplied at the back of the book. In general these test questions have been written in the interactive form that students will see in their real assessments

The emphasis in all tasks and test questions is on the practical application of the skills acquired.

If you have any comments about this book, please e-mail suedexter@bpp.com or write to Sue Dexter, Publishing Director, BPP Learning Media Ltd, BPP House, Aldine Place, London W12 8AA.

ASSESSMENT STRATEGY

The assessment will be set by the AAT and will be in two parts (Part one 60 minutes, Part two 120 minutes) and consist of a number of objective questions and mini project.

Part one consists of 27 objective questions, grouped into eight tasks, to assess learners' knowledge and understanding of key credit management concepts. Part two consists of a mini project assessing learners' skills in applying knowledge of credit and debt control. The project will be in two tasks: the assessment of credit status for the purposes of granting credit, and the assessment of an aged receivables' (debtors') analysis for the recommendation of actions and provisions.

The assessment material will normally be delivered online. Part one will be computer marked and part two will be assessed locally. Learners will be required to demonstrate competence in all parts of the assessment.

Alternatively, with guidance and support from training providers, learners can provide workplace evidence to be assessed locally by their training provider. The local assessor (training provider) will be required to ensure that all assessment criteria are covered.

Competency

Learners will be required to demonstrate competence in both sections of the assessment. For the purpose of assessment the competency level for AAT assessment is set at 70 per cent. The level descriptor in the table below describes the ability and skills students at this level must successfully demonstrate to achieve competence.

QCF Level descriptor	**Summary**
	Achievement at level 4 reflects the ability to identify and use relevant understanding, methods and skills to address problems that are well defined but complex and non-routine. It includes taking responsibility for overall courses of action as well as exercising autonomy and judgement within fairly broad parameters. It also reflects understanding of different perspectives or approaches within an area of study or work.
	Knowledge and understanding
	■ Practical, theoretical or technical understanding to address problems that are well defined but complex and non-routine
	■ Analyse, interpret and evaluate relevant information and ideas
	■ Be aware of the nature and approximate scope of the area of study or work
	■ Have an informed awareness of different perspectives or approaches within the area of study or work
	Application and action
	■ Address problems that are complex and non-routine while normally fairly well defined
	■ Identify, adapt and use appropriate methods and skills
	■ Initiate and use appropriate investigation to inform actions
	■ Review the effectiveness and appropriateness of methods, actions and results
	Autonomy and accountability
	■ Take responsibility for courses of action, including where relevant, responsibility for the work of others
	■ Exercise autonomy and judgement within broad but generally well-defined parameters

AAT UNIT GUIDE

Credit management and control

Introduction

For the purpose of assessment the Principles of Credit management and Control of debt and credit units will be combined. Please read this guidance in conjunction with the standards for the units.

This unit is all about the application and demonstration of the principles of Credit Management (Knowledge). Examinations will be entwined and the knowledge standards may well be assessed, by implication, in questions which require students to apply knowledge. For example the understanding and definitions of contract law may be examined by requiring students to analyse a doubtful debt and give advice on how to collect the debt.

This guidance details the learning outcomes and assessment criteria.

The purpose of the unit

This unit is about understanding the principles of credit and debt management in managing the granting of credit and collection of amounts outstanding from customers in an organisation. The learner will be able to give advice on the granting of credit, and also the collection of monies owed in compliance with relevant legislation, good practice and organisational policy. The learner will also be able to give advice on the management of debts and on methods which will minimise the risk to the organisation.

Terminology

The text uses international terminology throughout, with UK terms in brackets. This is to reflect the AAT's assessments which, from 2012, will use international terminology only.

Learning outcomes

There are two QCF units involved. Each is divided into component learning outcomes, which in turn comprise a number of assessment criteria.

QCF Unit	Learning outcome	Assessment criteria	Covered in chapter
Principles of credit management (Knowledge)	Understand how legislation impacts upon credit control	Explain the main features of contract laws and remedies for breach of contract in relation to the credit the organisation offers its customers Define the terms and conditions associated with contracts relating to the granting of credit Explain the importance of data protection legislation and how it applies to credit management Explain legal and administrative procedures for the collection of debts Explain the effect of bankruptcy and insolvency on organisations	3
	Understand how to prepare and use information from a variety of sources to manage the organisation's granting of credit	Explain the importance of liquidity management Identify the information requirements for credit control Identify sources of credit status and other related information Explain methods of analysing credit control information Identify a range of methods of analysing information on debtors	1

QCF Unit	Learning outcome	Assessment criteria	Covered in chapter
	Be aware of a range of techniques and methods of credit control that might be used within an organisation	Explain the reasons for offering discounts for prompt payment and identify the effect of offering such a discount Identify a range of methods for the collection and management of debts and explain the appropriateness of each method	4
Control of debt and credit (Skills)	Grant credit to customers within organisational guidelines	Evaluate the current credit status of customers and potential customers Agree credit terms with customers in accordance with the organisation's policies Open new accounts for those customers with an established credit status Agree changes to credit levels or credit terms with customers Discuss tactfully the reasons for refusing or extending credit with customers	2

QCF Unit	Learning outcome	Assessment criteria	Covered in chapter
	Manage the supply of credit	Regularly monitor and analyse information relating toreceivables' (debtors') accounts	5
		Promptly send information regarding significant outstanding accounts and potential bad debts to relevant individuals with the organisation	
		Negotiate with receivables in a courteous and professional manner and accurately record the outcome of negotiations	
		In accordance with organisational procedures select debt recovery methods appropriate individual outstanding receivables	
		Make recommendations to write off bad debts and make allowances (provisions) for doubtful debts based upon a realistic analysis of all known factors	

Delivery guidance: Principles of credit management

1. **Understand how legislation impacts upon credit control.**

   Candidates will need to demonstrate that they understand how legislation impacts upon the credit control function. Whilst the credit controller does not need to be a qualified lawyer there is some basic legislation which candidates need to understand and be able to define and explain.

1.1 **Explain the main features of contract law and remedies for breach of contract in relation to the credit the organisation offers its customers.**

In order to ensure that money is received for the sale of goods or the provision of services the credit controller needs to be able to explain the main features of contract law, which include offer and acceptance, remedies available in order to collect outstanding amounts, which include an action for price, and remedies available in the case of customer insolvency, which include retention of title claims.

The legislation that impacts upon credit control includes contract law. Candidates need to have knowledge and understanding and be able to define and explain the essential characteristics of a contract (including offer, acceptance and consideration).

Candidates need to explain the main documents which form the contract (written order from a customer) and those which are simply an invitation to treat (trade price list).

Other relevant legislation

Trade Descriptions Act – candidates need to understand that it is a criminal offence to make a false statement or to make a misleading statement. Candidates may have to comment on whether a scenario is in breach of this Act.

Unfair Contract Terms Act – candidates need to understand that unfair terms cannot be part of a contract.

Sale of Goods Act 1979 – candidates need to understand when the Sale of Goods Act applies, when title to the goods pass, what conditions can be attached and the key terms of "satisfactory quality", "fit for purpose", "as described".

Consumer Credit Act 1974 – candidates need to understand the key terms of the act.

Late Payment of Commercial Debts (Interest) Act 1998

Candidates may be required to define key terms of the above legislation.

Remedies for breach of contract

Candidates need to understand and be able to describe and explain the main remedies for breach of contract including damages and specific performance.

1.2 Define the terms and conditions associated with contracts relating to the granting of credit.

Candidates need to be able to define the terms and conditions associated with contracts including offer, acceptance, intention to create legal relations, consideration, capacity to create a contract, consent to the terms, legal and possible, void contracts, voidable contracts and unenforceable contracts.

1.3 Explain the importance of data protection legislation and how it applies to credit management.

Candidates need to be able to explain the importance of data protection legislation and how it affects both company and individual customers. Candidates need to understand that the Data Protection Act applies to individuals and not companies. Candidates need to be able to explain how the act applies to credit management for example, the security and use of data.

1.4 Explain legal and administrative procedures for the collection of debts.

Candidates need to be able to explain the administrative process for the collection of outstanding accounts. This process starts with the receipt of an order and finishes with the posting of the cash received from the customer. Candidates need to be able to explain the stages in the process and explain the importance of each stage and how earlier stages such as establishing the contract are fundamental to ensuring that customers pay on time or that action can be taken which will result in the successful collection of a debt.

Candidates need to be able to explain the legal and administrative procedures which must be followed for collecting amounts outstanding from customers.

These are

(1) Small claims court action

(2) County court action

(3) High court action

(4) Ways to enforce the judgment – garnishee order, warrant of execution, warrant of delivery, attachment of earnings, charging order

(5) The role of the debt collection agency

(6) The role of solicitors

1.5 Explain the effect of bankruptcy and insolvency on organisations.

Candidates need to be able to explain how the bankruptcy or insolvency of a customer may impact on the organisation. Candidates need to understand that supplying goods or services to a customer is an unsecured debt and that in the event of the insolvency of a customer often little or no money will be received in lieu of the amount outstanding. Candidates need to be able to explain the types of personal insolvency and company insolvency and what action can be taken.

2 Understand how to prepare and use information from a variety of sources to manage the organisation's granting of credit.

Candidates will need to demonstrate that they understand how to prepare and use information from various sources to manage the granting of credit.

The information used to assess credit can be either externally generated or internally generated. The main types of externally generated information are trade credit references, bank references, credit reference agency reports, statutory accounts, management accounts provided by the customer and credit circle meetings. The main types of internally generated information include trading history (for existing customers), information from the sales department, and reports generated from external information such as ratio calculations.

Candidates need to have an understanding of why this information is needed and explain how to use it. Candidates may be required to explain the usefulness of various types of information and explain how to select the most appropriate type to use in a given scenario. This learning outcome may also be assessed indirectly by requiring candidates to apply their understanding to a given scenario and recommend a course of action.

Key to the management of credit is the information available for the assessment of whether to grant credit in the first place. There is often a large range of data available and it is important to know the types of data, how it can be used and the integrity of the data.

2.1 Explain the importance of liquidity management.

Candidates need to be able to explain the importance of liquidity management and how an effective credit control function is fundamental to the liquidity of the business. For most businesses all their turnover is made on credit terms and therefore it is critical to manage the process in order to ensure that sales are only made to organisations which, it has been assessed, will pay to terms and that timely collection of these amounts is taken.

- Candidates need to be able to explain the importance of liquidity management and how an effective credit control function is fundamental to the liquidity of the business.

- Candidates need to be able to explain the difference between a cash sale and a credit sale and the risks associated with a credit sale.

- Candidates need to be able to explain the effect that increasing credit terms has on the cash flow of the business.

- Candidates may be required to explain the cost to the business of extending credit terms or giving cash discounts for prompt payment and its impact on liquidity management.

- Candidates need to be able to describe the main features of invoice discounting and factoring and explain how they can aid the liquidity management of the business. Credit insurance may be required as part of a factoring arrangement or may simply be another tool to aid liquidity management. Candidates may be required to explain the main features of credit insurance, how it aids credit control and its limitations.

2.2 Identify the information requirements for credit control.

Candidates need to be able to identify information required for credit control purposes. This information includes both internally generated and externally generated information. Candidates also need to be able to identify those requirements which are specific to a particular type of organisation.

- Candidates need to understand that a company has access to internal and external information and that different types of organisation will need to consider different types of information.

- Candidates need to be able to explain how to select and use various information provided.

- Candidates need to be able to explain the difference between the supply of goods and the supply of services and how the information requirements may be different.

Candidates may be required to explain why it is important to regularly monitor receivables' (debtors') accounts, explain what information should be monitored and how that information could be analysed.

2.3 Identify sources of credit status and other related information.

Candidates will need to be familiar with the types and structure of credit information. Candidates may be required to explain and describe the most appropriate type of information to be used in a particular case and explain how the information can be used in order to decide whether or not credit should be given. Below is the list of information which candidates need to be able to identify, describe and explain.

- Credit rating agencies reports
- Supplier references
- Bank references
- Statutory accounts filed at companies house
- Management accounts if available
- Information provided by colleagues
- Official publications

2.4 Explain methods of analysing credit control information.

Candidates need to be able to explain the following methods of analysing credit control information:

- Age analysis – an explanation of what an age analysis is, the importance of an accurate and timely age analysis, how to use an aged analysis and why it is needed in order to efficiently manage credit.

- Average periods of credit given and received – an explanation of what is an average period of credit and how a rapidly expanding turnover can affect the measure of the average period of credit.

■ Incidence of bad and doubtful debts – an explanation of a bad debt and a doubtful debt and how each affects the cash flow of the organisation.

2.5 Identify a range of methods of analysing information on debtors.

Candidates need to be able to identify a range of methods of analysing information on debtors including:

■ Aged analysis
■ Trading history
■ Average periods of credit
■ 80/20 rule
■ Materiality
■ Status reports

3. Be aware of a range of techniques and methods of credit control that may be used within an organisation.

Candidates will need to be aware of the generic credit control process and the techniques and methods that may be used to efficiently collect outstanding customer accounts. Candidates may be required to explain how to communicate with customers, when to communicate with customers, when to instruct a debt collection agency, when to instruct solicitors and when to issue proceedings.

Candidates need to be aware that there is a range of techniques and methods for the collection of outstanding monies. These include the correct application of contract law, various ways to communicate with the customer and various time frames for this communication. The type of communication will depend on the nature of the goods or services. It is unlikely that a stationery company will meet face to face to discuss payment terms whereas a defence contractor with a multi million pound order is likely to have detailed face to face meetings to agree prices and payment schedules probably with interim payments during the contract.

3.1 Explain the reasons for offering discounts for prompt payment and identify the effects of offering such a discount.

Candidates need to explain how offering discounts aids the liquidity of the organisation and explain how discounts can improve cash flow of the organisation. Candidates need also to be able to explain the cost of offering discounts and identify the effects.

3.2 Identify a range of methods for the collection and management of debts and explain the appropriateness of each method.

Candidates need to be able to identify methods for the collection and management of debts and explain the appropriateness of each method. These methods include

■ Clear credit control policy

- Written communication (the sending of invoices, statements, solicitor's letters)
- The use of telecommunications (contact via the telephone, email, internet)
- Restricting future trade (placing on stop), reducing credit limits, reducing payment terms
- The use of third parties such as debt collection agencies, factoring companies, credit insurance companies, solicitors
- Small claims summons, County Court summons, High Court summons
- The use of the Late Payment of Commercial Debts (Interest) Act 1998

Delivery guidance: Control of debt and credit

1 Grant credit to customers within organisational guidelines.

Successful candidates will be able to grant credit to customers by following good practice, reviewing customer information, considering a range of factors having particular regard to organisational guidelines. Candidates need to be able to select and use a range of tools when granting credit.

1.1 Evaluate the current credit status of customers and potential customers.

Candidates will be required to evaluate the current credit status of existing customers and potential customers. This process will be undertaken by using a variety of information collected from both internal and external sources. The information which may be provided for evaluation include the following:

- Credit rating agencies reports
- Supplier references
- Bank references
- Statutory accounts filed at companies house
- Management accounts
- Credit circle reports
- Information provided by colleagues
- Official publications.

Candidates will be required to extract relevant information and possibly prepare calculations based upon the information provided. Candidates will be required to prepare ratio calculations based upon published financial information and management accounting information. Candidates may be required to explain and use ratios to evaluate credit status. Candidates may also be required to use a credit scoring system where they have to calculate a credit score based upon a range of performance indicators.

The following financial performance indicators may be assessed.

- Liquidity indicators

  - Current ratio
  - Quick ratio
  - Receivable (debtor) days
  - Payable (creditor) days
  - Inventory (stock) turnover
  - Working capital cycle

- Profitability indicators

  - Gross profit margin
  - Net profit margin
  - Interest cover
  - Return on capital employed

- Debt indicators

  - Gearing ratio – total debt (short term and long term) / total debt plus equity

  - Short term debt ratio – short term debt as a percentage of total debt

- Cash flow indicators

  - EBITDA – earnings before interest, tax, depreciation and amortisation

  - EBITDA interest cover – EBITDA/interest payable (income statement (profit and loss account)) or EBITDA/ interest paid (cash flow statement, if available)

  - EBITDA to total debt

1.2 Agree credit terms with customers in accordance with the organisation's policies.

Once the customer's information has been assessed, credit terms can be agreed. Candidates may be given the organisation's policy and required to set appropriate terms. This may include size of any credit limit and terms of payment of invoices as well as terms such as retention of title. Candidates may be required to decide on the size of a credit limit based upon the expected orders notified by the sales department. For example, a new customer may have passed the evaluation stage and the sales department expects to receive weekly orders of £5,000. Clearly a credit limit of £10,000 will not be sufficient.

Credit insurance may be used and this may inform the decision as to whether to agree credit and set appropriate levels. Candidates need to understand credit insurance and may be required to explain a given credit insurance opinion. Candidates may also be required to advise management on whether to trade with a new customer where credit insurance has been refused.

1.3 Open new accounts for those customers with an established credit status.

Candidates may be provided with a credit control policy and procedure for the opening of accounts for new customers. Candidates may be required to explain the policy and procedure and the reasons for the stages or they may be presented with a selection on new customers and required to apply the policy to decide which new customers should be given credit.

1.4 Agree changes to credit levels or credit terms with customers.

Candidates may be required to agree changes to current levels of credit in response from a request from a customer or salesman. Examinations may provide additional information and require candidates to assess whether the credit levels or terms should be changed. For example a new customer may be given a £10,000 credit limit and after trading for several months place an order for £15,000. The decision will depend on an assessment to include the trading history of the customer and whether they have kept within their current limit and paid to terms.

1.5 Discuss tactfully the reasons for refusing or extending credit with customers

Candidates may be required to draft a response to a customer's request for credit where this request has been refused. Candidates may be required to explain how the refusal of credit should be made and what should be included in a refusal. The refusal should be polite and explain the reasons for refusal and explain what the company could do to improve their chances of obtaining credit in future including trading on a cash basis to establish a trading history.

2. Manage the supply of credit.

Candidates need to be able to manage the supply of credit and prepare information to aid the collection of outstanding amounts on a timely basis.

2.1 Regularly monitor and analyse information relating to receivables' (debtors') accounts.

Candidates may be required to monitor receivables' accounts including the preparation of an aged receivables' report, compliance with payment terms, monitor and implement the organisations policy in respect of placing accounts on hold.

Candidates may be required to analyse an aged receivables' report and make recommendations as to the action to be taken for individual accounts. Candidates may also be provided with a credit control policy and required to apply this policy to a range of receivables' accounts stating the action to be taken.

2.2 Promptly send information regarding significant outstanding accounts and potential bad debts to relevant individuals within the organisation.

Candidates may be required to prepare an email/ memo, in response to a specific request or as part of the monitoring of receivables (debtors), regarding significant outstanding amounts and suggest actions to taken and allowances (provisions) to be made. This could include the suggestion to place an account on hold, instruct a debt collection agency or issue legal proceedings and to make an allowance.

2.3 Negotiate with receivables (debtors) in a courteous and professional manner and accurately record the outcome of negotiations.

Candidates may be required to prepare a telephone brief or letter which outlines the discussions/ negotiations which have been entered into with a customer. For example, a customer may owe an amount of money and is offering to pay by instalments. It may have been decided by the credit controller that the customer will be allowed to pay over say three or four instalments and that legal proceedings will not be entered into unless the instalments are not paid.

2.4 In accordance with organisational procedures select debt recovery methods appropriate to individual outstanding receivables (debtors).

Candidates may be given an aged receivables' report which requires analysis and recommended actions. Candidates need to be able to consider the aged receivables' analysis and supplementary information in order to select an appropriate recovery method. Methods include a telephone call, letter or statement, use of a debt collection agency, legal proceedings or possible negotiating with an insolvent company or insolvency practitioner.

2.5 Make recommendations to write off bad debts and make allowances (provisions) for doubtful debts based upon a realistic analysis of all known factors.

Candidates will be required to recommend which outstanding amounts should be written off and allowances that should be made.

chapter 1:
MANAGING THE GRANTING OF CREDIT

chapter coverage 📖

In this initial chapter of the Text we consider the importance of liquidity management and how an effective credit control function is fundamental to the liquidity of a business. In the next few chapters we will examine the granting of credit, the monitoring of receivables (debtors) and the collection of debts. However, we start with a consideration of the overall role and purpose of credit control.

The topics covered are:

✎ What is meant by liquidity

✎ The role of credit control

✎ Credit control policy

✎ Terms and conditions of credit granted

✎ Assessment of credit status

LIQUIDITY

LIQUIDITY is the ability of a company to pay its suppliers on time, meet its operational costs such as wages and salaries and to pay any longer-term outstanding amounts such as loan repayments. Adequate liquidity is often a key factor in contributing to the success or failure of a business. The liquidity of a business is the availability of cash or assets which can easily be converted into cash, therefore liquidity is not just about holding cash in hand or in a bank current account as there are also other liquid assets. These include:

- Deposit account balances
- Short-term investments which can easily be sold and converted into cash

Liquidity is a measure of how safe the business is in terms of its cash availability. Even if a business is profitable it must have enough cash to pay amounts due when they become payable.

It is important to realise that although cash is the most liquid of assets, it is part of the working capital of the business and that the time taken to convert inventory (stock) and trade receivables (debtors) into cash and the time taken to pay suppliers affects the liquidity position of the business. Therefore it is important to appreciate that an effective credit control function is fundamental to the liquidity of the business.

THE ROLE OF CREDIT CONTROL

Cash and credit transactions

We must be quite clear about the distinction between transactions which are for cash and those which are on credit.

A CASH TRANSACTION is one that takes place either with coins and notes, a cheque, a credit card or a debit card. Cash transactions are basically those for which money will be available in the business bank account almost immediately, once the amounts have been paid into the bank.

A CREDIT TRANSACTION is one where the receipt or the payment is delayed for a period of time, as agreed between the two parties to the transaction. Many business sales and purchases are made on credit whereby the goods are delivered or received now but payment is agreed to be received or made in say 30 or 60 days' time.

Granting credit

The decision as to whether or not to grant credit to customers is an important commercial decision. The granting of credit to customers means that they will be able to delay payment for goods purchased but this delay is an important marketing aspect of business that almost always leads to a greater level of sales.

The benefit of offering credit to customers is therefore additional sales and accompanying profits. However, there are also costs involved in offering credit:

- Interest cost – if money is received later from customers then the business is either losing interest, as it does not have the money in its bank account, or is being charged more interest on any overdraft balance

- Bad debts cost – if sales are made for cash then the money is received at the time of the sale, but with a credit sale there is always some risk that the goods will be despatched but never paid for

Despite these costs of granting credit, most businesses trade on a credit basis with at least some of their customers due to the benefits of additional sales and competitive advantage.

Credit control function

As we have seen there are two main costs involved in trading with customers on credit, the interest cost and the bad debts cost. The role of the credit control function is to minimise these costs.

In a small organisation the credit control function may consist of a single member of the accounting operation, but in a larger institution the credit control function may be an entire department.

There are two main stages in the credit control function:

- The ordering cycle
- The collection cycle

The ordering cycle

The ORDERING CYCLE can be illustrated:

Customer places
order
|
Customer credit
status established
|
Customer offered
credit
|
Goods despatched
|
Goods delivered
|
Invoice despatched

The credit control function is directly involved with the earlier elements of the ordering cycle – the establishment of the credit status of the customer and the offering of credit to the customer (both of these areas are dealt with in Chapter 2 of this Text).

Although the credit control function is not normally involved in the despatch or invoicing of the goods, they will need access to the documents involved with these activities.

The collection cycle

The COLLECTION CYCLE starts where the ordering cycle finishes:

Customer receives
invoice
|
Statement sent
to customer
|
Reminder letters
sent to customer
|
Telephone calls
to customer
|
Cash received

These elements form a major part of the credit control function's role and are dealt with in Chapter 5 of this Text.

Supply of good and of services

A business may be supplying either goods or services to a customer. A manufacturing or wholesale organisation will be selling goods to another business, whereas a service company such as an accountancy firm or a cleaning contractor will be providing services. Whatever the type of company, they are likely to be offering credit to their customers.

Task 1

What are the main elements of the ordering cycle for goods to be sold on credit?

CREDIT CONTROL POLICY

Each business has its own credit control policies and procedures but they will all tend to cover the following areas:

- Assessment of credit standing of new customers
- Assessment of credit standing of existing customers
- Customers exceeding credit limits
- Terms and conditions of credit granted
- Payment methods allowed
- Collection procedures

TERMS AND CONDITIONS OF CREDIT GRANTED

The credit terms offered to a customer are part of the contract between the business and the customer (see Chapter 3 of this Text) and as such should normally be in writing. The TERMS OF CREDIT are the precise agreements with the customer as to how and when payment for the goods should be made. The most basic element of the terms of credit is the time period in which the customer should pay the invoice for the goods. There are a variety of ways of expressing these terms:

- Net 10/14/30 days – payment is due 10 or 14 or 30 days after delivery of the goods
- Weekly credit – all goods must be paid for by a specified date in the following week
- Half-monthly credit – all goods delivered in one-half of the month must be paid for by a specified date in the following half-month
- Monthly credit – all goods delivered in one month must be paid for by a specified date in the following month

Settlement discounts

In some cases customers may be offered a SETTLEMENT DISCOUNT or CASH DISCOUNT for payment within a certain period which is shorter than the stated credit period. The details of such discounts are considered in Chapter 4 of this Text.

The terms of such a settlement discount may be expressed as follows:

Net 30 days, 2% discount for payment within 14 days

This means that the basic payment terms are that the invoice should be paid within 30 days of its date but that if payment is made within 14 days of the invoice date a 2% discount can be deducted. It is up to the customer to decide whether or not to take advantage of the settlement discount offered.

Task 2

If an invoice includes the term "net monthly", what does this mean?

A   Invoice must be paid in the month of issue of invoice.

B   Invoice must be paid the month after the invoice date.

C   Invoice must be paid within a month of the invoice date.

D   Invoice must be paid net of any discount within a month of the invoice date.

ASSESSMENT OF CREDIT STATUS

As stated earlier, the decision to grant credit to a customer is an extremely important commercial judgment. The granting of credit to a customer normally leads to continued and possibly increasing sales to that customer. However, there are also risks involved:

- The customer may extend the period of credit by not paying within the stated credit period and therefore deprive the seller of cash which may be vital for the purposes of cash flow.

- The customer may never pay at all if, for example, they went into liquidation and unsecured creditors received nothing (see Chapter 3 of this Text).

Therefore, a very important role of the credit controller is to be able to assess the credit status of customers to determine whether or not they should be granted a period of credit, how long that credit period should be and what their credit limit should be. This role applies not only to new customers of the business but also to established customers who may wish to increase their credit limit or renegotiate their credit terms.

What is the credit controller looking for?

When evaluating the credit status of a customer the credit controller is looking for a client who will pay within the stated credit terms and whose business will remain solvent. Some customers will be low risk as they are safe, liquid businesses. Others will be higher risk due to the nature of the occupation they are in or the way in which the enterprise is run. Higher risk customers however may also be highly profitable customers.

Accordingly, the credit controller needs to assess the risk of the customer to determine whether the risk is acceptable for the sake of the additional sales that will be made.

Task 3

What are the risks of granting credit to a customer?

Assessment process

The process of assessing a customer's credit status and the actions that follow can be illustrated:

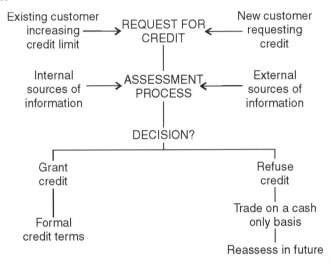

Sources of information

When assessing the credit status of either an established or a new customer there are a variety of sources of information that the credit controller can draw upon, some are external to the business and others are internal.

Remember that the credit controller is concerned about the customer's ability and tendency to pay within the stated credit terms and also that the customer will remain solvent. No one source of information can guarantee either of these but there are a variety of sources which can be considered and all of the information can be pooled together for a final decision on credit status to be made.

The sources of information available for assessing a customer's credit status include the following:

External sources

- Bank reference
- Trade reference
- Credit reference agencies
- Companies House (for filed financial statements)
- Management accounts from the customer
- Media publications
- The internet

Internal sources

- Staff knowledge
- Customer visits
- Financial analysis of either external published financial statements or internal management accounts provided by the customer

For an established customer their credit record can be assessed by analysis of the business's aged receivables' (debtors') listing (see Chapter 5 of this Text).

All of these sources of potential information for assessing the credit status of a customer are considered in detail in the following chapters.

Task 4

Indicate whether each of the following sources of information for assessing the credit status of customers is internal or external:

Credit reference agency	
Staff knowledge	
Financial analysis of customer accounts	
Bank reference	
The internet	

CHAPTER OVERVIEW

- Adequate liquidity is often a key factor in contributing to the success or failure of a business. The liquidity of a business is the availability of cash or assets which can easily be converted into cash.

- The benefit of offering credit to customers is the likely increase in sales. However there are also costs of lost interest and potential bad debts. The role of the credit control function is to minimise these costs.

- The credit control function is involved in the ordering cycle in establishing customer credit status and offering credit terms and throughout the collection cycle.

- Every business will have its own credit control policies, terms and conditions regarding how and when payment is to be made by credit customers.

- When evaluating a customer's credit status the concerns are that the customer will pay within the stated credit terms and that their business will remain solvent.

- When either a potential new customer requests credit or an existing customer requests an increase in credit limit, the credit controller will make use of internal and external information about the customer, in order to determine whether or not the request should be granted.

Keywords

Liquidity – the ability of the business to pay its suppliers on time and to meet other operational costs

Cash transaction – one that takes place either with coins and notes, a cheque, a credit card or a debit card

Credit transaction – one where the receipt or the payment is delayed for a period of time, as agreed between the two parties to the transaction

Credit control function – the person or department responsible for minimising the interest and bad debt cost involved in trading with customers on credit

Ordering cycle – the processes from when a customer places an order to the sending out of the sales invoice

Collection cycle – the processes from the sending out of the sales invoice to the receipt of cash from a customer

Terms of credit – the precise agreements as to how and when a customer is due to pay for goods purchased

Settlement/Cash discount – a discount offered for payment within a shorter period than the stated credit terms

TEST YOUR LEARNING

Test 1

Which of the following are the main costs of making sales on credit?

(i)   Loss of customers
(ii)   Loss of interest
(iii) Loss of goodwill
(iv)   Bad debts

A   (i) and (ii)
B   (ii) and (iii)
C   (i) and (iv)
D   (ii) and (iv)

Test 2

Which of the following is not a main element of the collection cycle which will be part of the role of the credit control function within an organisation?

A   Customer receives reminder letter
B   Customer receives statement
C   Customer receives invoice
D   Customer places order

Test 3

A company sets a credit policy of normal payment within 14 days but a 3% settlement discount for payment within seven days.

How would this policy be expressed on an invoice?

Test 4

A potential new customer approaches your business with a request for credit facilities.

Which of the following are processes that would be followed by the credit controller?

(i)   Analysis of external information
(ii)   Analysis of aged receivables' (debtors') listing
(iii) Analysis of payment history
(iv)   Analysis of internally produced ratios
(v)   Communication of decision to customers

A   (i), (ii), (iii), (v)
B   (ii), (iii), (iv)
C   (i), (iv), (v)
D   All of them

chapter 2:
GRANTING CREDIT TO CUSTOMERS

chapter coverage 📖

In this chapter we consider how to evaluate the current credit status of existing customers and potential customers. This process will be undertaken by using a variety of information collected from both internal and external sources. You will need to be able to extract relevant information and to prepare calculations based upon the information provided. Once the customer's information has been assessed then the credit terms can be agreed. Alternatively, it may be necessary to refuse credit at this stage and this must be communicated to the customer.

The topics covered are:

✍ Sources of information

✍ External sources of information

✍ Internal sources of information

✍ Financial ratio analysis

✍ Making a credit assessment

✍ Communication of credit assessment decision

✍ Refusal of credit

SOURCES OF INFORMATION

As stated in Chapter 1, when assessing the credit status of either an established customer or a new customer there are a variety of sources of information that the credit controller can draw upon – some are external to the business and others are internal.

Remember that the credit controller is concerned about the customer's ability and tendency to pay within the stated credit terms and also that the customer will remain solvent. No one source of information can guarantee either of these but there are a variety of sources which can be considered and all of the information can be pooled together for a final decision on credit status to be made.

EXTERNAL SOURCES OF INFORMATION

If the credit controller wishes to assess the solvency of the customer and the likelihood of them paying within the stated credit period then two of the most obvious potential sources of information are the customer's bank and other suppliers that the customer uses.

Consequently, if a new customer approaches the business with an order and a request for credit, it is normal practice for the credit controller to ask for a BANK REFERENCE and normally two TRADE REFERENCES. In order to do this the business will make a request to the new customer for details of their bank and for details of two other suppliers with whom they regularly trade. This may be done in a letter to the potential customer or more usually by sending the customer a standard CREDIT APPLICATION FORM.

HOW IT WORKS

The fuel division of SC Fuel and Glass has been approached by a new customer, Haven Engineering Ltd who would like to place regular orders with the fuel division for approximately £15,000 a month and wish to trade on credit with SC.

SC Fuel and Glass has a standard credit application form which the credit controller sends to the finance director of Haven Engineering Ltd.

CREDIT APPLICATION FORM

SC FUEL AND GLASS
CRAWLEY RD
CRAWLEY
CR7 JN9
Tel: 01453 732166 Fax: 01453 732177

Business name   ....
Address   ....
Telephone   ....
E-mail   ....

Amount of credit required   £ .... monthly
£ .... in total

You are hereby authorised to contact the parties named below for further information.

Signed .... Position .... Date ....
Signed .... Position .... Date ....

Bank reference

Bank name   ....
Bank address   ....
Account name   ....

Trade references

Name   .... Name   ....
Address   .... Address   ....

Bank references

Once the potential customer has provided details of their bank and authorised them to release the information required, a reference can be requested from the bank.

HOW IT WORKS

SC Fuel and Glass has received the completed credit application form back from Haven Engineering Ltd with a request for £15,000 of credit per month. SC Fuel and Glass will now write to Haven Engineering Ltd's bank:

"Do you consider Haven Engineering Ltd to be good for the figure of £15,000 trade credit per month?"

Bank replies to reference requests

The next stage will be a reply received from the bank which must be interpreted. The banks have two considerations when replying to a request for a reference regarding a customer:

- Confidentiality of the customer's affairs

- Accusations of negligence from the recipient of the reference if the reference proves to be wrong

As a consequence, bank references tend to all be worded in a similar manner with a well-known "real" meaning. Examples of the most commonly used phrases as a reply to a request for a credit reference and their "real" meaning are as follows:

Bank's reply	Real meaning
The customer's credit for £X is:	
Undoubted	The best type of reference – the customer should be of low risk for the figures stated
Considered good for your purposes	Probably OK and a reasonable risk but not as good as undoubted
Should prove good for your figures	Not quite as certain as the other two and therefore warrants further investigation
Well constituted business with capital seeming to be fully employed: we do not consider that the directors/owners would undertake a commitment they could not fulfil	Not very hopeful – this probably means the business has cash flow problems and credit should not be extended to them
Unable to speak for your figures	The worst – the bank seems to believe that the business is already overstretched – definitely no credit to be granted

Trade references

Once the business has received details of trade referees from the potential customer, it is standard practice to send out a letter asking for information from them.

HOW IT WORKS

Haven Engineering Ltd has provided SC with details of two trade referees. The credit controller now completes a standard letter to each of these referees. Here is one of those letters:

SC FUEL AND GLASS
CRAWLEY RD
CRAWLEY
CR7 JN9
Tel: 01453 732166 Fax: 01453 732177

Credit controller
Peterhay Systems
Hove Park Estate
Brighton BR4 7HD

Date:

We have received a request for credit from Haven Engineering Ltd quoting yourselves as a referee. We would be grateful if you could answer the following questions, and return this form in the stamped addressed envelope enclosed.

How long has the customer been trading with you?	.... years .... mths
Your credit terms with customer per month	£
Period of credit granted	....
Payment record	Prompt/occasionally late/slow
Have you ever suspended credit to the customer?	Yes/No
If yes – when and for how long?	....
Any other relevant information	....

Thank you for your assistance.

Yours faithfully

Tom Hunt
Credit controller

Problems with trade references

When replies are received from trade referees they should be fairly easy to interpret, as the questions asked are fairly direct. However, care should be taken not to necessarily take every trade reference at face value.

- Some firms deliberately pay two or three suppliers promptly in order to use them as trade referees, while delaying payment to their other suppliers.

- The trade referee may be connected or influenced in some way by the potential customer, for example it may be a business owned by one of the directors of the customer.

- The trade referee given may not be particularly strict themselves regarding credit control, therefore their replies might not be typical – the genuine nature of the trade referee should be checked.

- Even if the reference is genuine and favourable, it may be that trade with this supplier is on a much smaller basis or on different credit terms to that being sought by the customer.

Task 1

What would be the typical response of a credit controller to a bank reference which read "unable to speak for your figures"?

A Grant credit

B Further investigation of external information

C Do not grant credit

D Further investigation of internal information

Credit reference agencies

CREDIT REFERENCE AGENCIES are commercial organisations which specialise in providing a variety of information regarding the credit status of companies and individuals. These agencies have large databases of information and can provide historic information such as financial reports, directors' details, payment history, any insolvency proceedings or bankruptcy orders for individuals, and bankers' opinions. They will sometimes also provide a credit rating.

Examples of credit reference agencies in the UK are Equifax, Dun and Bradstreet and Experian.

Such credit reference agency reports are a useful source of information for the credit controller but it must be borne in mind that they are a summary of only some of the information about the customer and that they may be based upon out-of-date historic data.

Credit circles

CREDIT CIRCLES are groups of companies who are usually competitors which means that they tend to have customers or potential customers in common. Often such groups of companies will meet formally every few months to discuss relevant matters. However, the members of the credit circle tend to remain in touch on a more informal basis, by telephone or e-mail, in order to either request or give information on potential new customers or, possibly, on changing payment patterns from existing customers.

Companies House

If the potential customer is a company then it must file certain financial information regarding its annual accounts and directors with Companies House. This information can be accessed by anyone but is unlikely to be particularly up-to-date, as companies need not file their annual accounts until some considerable time after their year end.

Financial information that is far more useful, if it can be obtained, is internal management accounts of the prospective customer and these will tend to be much more current. However, they do have the drawback of having no set format and, more importantly, not being independently checked by an external auditor.

Publications

More up-to-date information can also often be found about a customer from various media sources. Newspapers such as the *Financial Times* run articles on many companies, as do various trade journals for companies in particular lines of business.

Internet

The internet is a powerful tool for information and by running a search on a company name you may be able to find a number of useful articles and updates.

INTERNAL SOURCES OF INFORMATION

Internal sources of information about an existing or potential customer can be both information from employees within the organisation and information that is analysed by employees. In most cases the employees of a business will have little information about potential customers but should have a good level of knowledge of existing customers.

Existing customers

So far in this chapter we have been considering the scenario of a new, potential customer requesting credit facilities but the credit control function will also have to deal with existing customers requesting an increase in their credit limit or other changes to their credit terms. (This is considered further in Chapter 5 of this Text.) In such cases there will be employees within the organisation who have detailed knowledge of these customers.

Sales staff   The sales staff deal with customers on a regular basis. They are likely to have opinions as to how well the customer is doing, how efficient they are or any financial difficulties they may be in.

Sales ledger staff   The sales ledger staff deal with the recording and monitoring of invoices and receipts from receivables (debtors). They will be able to provide information about the payment history of the customer and the customer's adherence to current credit limits.

Customer visits

Some internal staff, particularly the sales team, are likely to pay fairly regular visits to the customer's premises and they should be able to provide feedback as to how prosperous and efficient the customer appears to be.

Financial analysis

One of the most useful sources of internal information however is an analysis of the existing or potential customer's financial statements (or possibly management accounts) and the preparation of relevant accounting ratios.

FINANCIAL RATIO ANALYSIS

The purpose of analysing the financial statements for credit control assessment is to find indicators of the customer's performance and position in four main areas:

- Profitability indicators
- Liquidity indicators
- Debt indicators
- Cash flow indicators

In general terms this analysis is only useful if it is carried out over a period of time, analysing financial statements for at least the last three years to determine any trends in business performance.

You may have already come across financial ratios in your earlier studies but we briefly consider the relevant ratios for credit control purposes below.

Profitability ratios

If credit is to be granted to a new customer or the credit limit of an existing customer increased, then one major concern will be the profitability of that customer. If the customer is not profitable in the long term then they will eventually go out of business and this may mean a loss, in the form of a bad debt, if they have been granted credit.

The main profitability ratios which will give indicators of the customer's long-term profitability are:

- Gross profit margin
- Net profit margin
- Return on capital employed
- Net asset turnover

Gross profit margin

$$\frac{\text{Gross profit}}{\text{Revenue}} \times 100\%$$

This gives an indication of how profitable the trading activities of the business are. This would be expected to remain fairly constant or increase over time.

Net profit margin

$$\frac{\text{Net profit}}{\text{Revenue}} \times 100\%$$

The net profit is profit after all expenses have been deducted and therefore indicates the overall profitability of the business. The usual profit figure to use is the operating profit. As efficiencies are introduced, this ratio should gradually increase over time or at the very least remain constant.

Return on capital employed (ROCE)

$$\frac{\text{Net profit}}{\text{Capital employed (net assets)}} \times 100\%$$

This is the overall profit indicator showing the profit as a percentage of the capital employed or the net assets of the business. This should increase or remain constant over time.

CAPITAL EMPLOYED is share capital, reserves and long-term debt but can also be measured as the net asset total of the business.

Net asset turnover

$$\frac{\text{Revenue}}{\text{Capital employed (net assets)}}$$

This ratio, measured as the number of times that revenue represents net assets, shows the efficiency of the use of the net assets of the business and, together with the net profit margin, helps to explain any change in return on capital employed.

Task 2

A company has a gross profit of £152,000 and operating profit of £76,000. Share capital is £200,000, reserves total £188,000 and there is a long-term loan of £100,000.

Calculate the company's return on capital employed.

	%
Return on capital employed	

Liquidity ratios

The purpose of calculating liquidity ratios is to provide indicators of the short-term and medium-term stability and solvency of the business. Can the business pay its debts when they fall due?

Liquidity indicators can be considered in total by the calculation of two overall liquidity ratios:

- Current ratio
- Quick ratio or acid test ratio

Liquidity and working capital management can also be examined by looking at the individual elements of the working capital of the business and calculating various turnover ratios:

- Inventory (stock) turnover
- Receivables' (debtors') turnover
- Payables' (creditors') turnover

Current ratio

$$\frac{\text{Current assets}}{\text{Current liabilities}}$$

This is a measure of whether current assets are sufficient to pay off current liabilities. It is sometimes stated that the ideal ratio is 2:1 but this will depend upon the type of business.

Quick ratio/acid test ratio

$$\frac{\text{Current assets} - \text{inventory (stock)}}{\text{Current liabilities}}$$

Inventory is removed from the current assets in this measure of liquidity, as it tends to take longer to turn into cash than other current assets. It is sometimes stated that the ideal ratio is 1:1 but again this is dependent upon the type of business.

Inventory (stock) turnover

$$\frac{\text{Inventory (stock)}}{\text{Cost of sales}} \times 365 \text{ days}$$

This measures how many days on average inventory is held before it is sold. This will depend upon the type of inventory but should ideally not increase significantly over time.

Receivables' (debtors') turnover

$$\frac{\text{Trade receivables (debtors)}}{\text{Sales}} \times 365 \text{ days}$$

This measures how many days on average it takes for receivables to pay. This will depend upon the type of business and the credit terms that are offered. Ideally, it should be around the average credit period offered to credit customers and similar to the time taken to pay suppliers.

Payables' (creditors') turnover

$$\frac{\text{Trade payables (creditors)}}{\text{Purchases}} \times 365 \text{ days}$$

This measures how many days on average the business takes to pay its trade payables. This is of direct relevance as it will give an indication of how long a period of credit the business normally takes from its suppliers.

Very often the purchases figure is not available from the financial statements and consequently cost of sales is used as an approximation.

Working capital cycle

The WORKING CAPITAL CYCLE or OPERATING CYCLE measures the period of time from when cash is paid out for raw materials until the time cash is received in from customers for goods sold.

(a) A firm buys raw materials, probably on credit.

(b) It holds the raw materials for some time in stores before they are issued to the production department and turned into finished goods.

(c) The finished goods may be kept in a warehouse for some time before they are eventually sold to customers.

(d) By this time, the firm will probably have paid for the raw materials purchased.

(e) If customers buy the goods on credit, it will be some time before the cash from the sales is eventually received.

The working capital cycle or operating cycle of a business in days is calculated as follows:

	Days
Inventory (stock) turnover period	X
Receivables' (debtors') turnover period	X
	X
Less: payables' (creditors') turnover period	(X)
Working capital cycle	X

Task 3

A company has sales of £980,000 and cost of sales of £686,000. Inventory (stock) at the year-end is £77,000, receivables (debtors) are £130,000 and payables (creditors) are £89,000.

Calculate the inventory turnover, receivables' turnover and payables' turnover figures in days.

	Days
Inventory turnover	
Receivables' turnover	
Payables' turnover	

Gearing ratios

When assessing a customer's credit status the credit controller will also be concerned with the longer-term stability of the business. One area of anxiety here is the amount of long term debt in the business's capital structure and its ability to service this debt by paying the periodic interest charges. The two main measures of this longer-term position are:

- Gearing ratio
- Interest cover

Gearing ratio

$$\frac{\text{Long term debt}}{\text{Capital employed}} \times 100\%$$

The gearing ratio is a measure of the proportion of interest-bearing debt to the total capital of the business. The capital employed or total capital of the business is usually defined as total debt plus equity.

The gearing ratio is often stated as ideal at 50% or less, although this will again vary between different industries and different businesses. The higher the figure the more risky the company may appear to be.

Interest cover

$$\frac{\text{Profit before interest}}{\text{Interest payable}}$$

The interest cover is calculated as the number of times that the interest could have been paid; it represents the margin of safety between the profits earned and the interest that must be paid to service the debt capital.

Cash flow indicators

In most of the calculations so far, the profit before interest figure from the income statement (profit and loss account) has been used in order to calculate various ratios. However, there are many users of accounts who believe that this figure is subject to management and accounting policies, so a further figure of EBITDA is often used in calculations. This is earnings before interest, tax, depreciation and amortisation and means taking the earnings before profit and tax figure and adding back any depreciation and amortisation charges.

It is argued that using this figure removes the subjective figures of depreciation and amortisation from the profit figure and gives a closer approximation to the underlying cash flows. This figure can then be used to calculate a number of further ratios which can be useful in assessing the cash flow situation of a business.

EBITDA interest cover

$$\frac{\text{EBITDA}}{\text{Interest payable}}$$

This is the same calculation as for interest cover but using EBITDA instead of profit before interest.

EBITDA to total debt

$$\frac{\text{EBITDA}}{\text{Total debt}} \times 100\%$$

This is a measure of the profits/cash flows available in comparison with the total debt of the company. It can give an indication of the ease with which the company can service its debt commitments from operations.

Task 4

A company has share capital of £200,000, reserves totalling £188,000 and a long-term loan of £100,000. The net profit for the year is £45,000, after deducting depreciation of £12,000 and interest of £6,000.

Calculate the company's gearing ratio, interest cover and EBITDA based interest cover

	Workings	
Gearing ratio		
Interest cover		
EBITDA based interest cover		

MAKING A CREDIT ASSESSMENT

So far in this chapter we have considered a number of internal and external sources of information available to the credit controller in his attempt to assess the current credit status of an existing or potential customer. It is likely that the credit controller will review most if not all of these sources of information and then use the information gathered to make a decision about the customer's credit status.

This may be a clear cut judgement where the bank reference is favourable, the trade references are sound and the analysis of the financial statements indicate a profitable and liquid business. Such a business would appear to be low risk and should be granted credit.

At the other end of the scale the bank and trade references may be unsatisfactory and an assessment of the financial statements may indicate problems with profitability and liquidity. This is a high risk business and trade should probably only be carried out on a cash basis.

Conflicting information

However, in many scenarios, the situation may not be as clear cut. The bank reference may be reasonable and the trade references viewed as sound but the analysis of the financial statements may indicate areas of concern. Alternatively the financial statements may appear reliable but the trade references are for much lower amounts of credit than the customer is asking for.

In circumstances such as these the credit controller must assess the conflicting information and determine the best course of action.

HOW IT WORKS

Tom Hunt, the credit controller at SC Fuel and Glass, is considering the request for £15,000 a month of credit facilities for Haven Engineering Ltd. The following references have now been received:

Bank reference

Haven Engineering Ltd – should prove good for your figures.

Trade references

SC FUEL AND GLASS
CRAWLEY RD
CRAWLEY
CR7 JN9
Tel: 01453 732166 Fax: 01453 732177

Credit controller
Peterhay Systems
Hove Park Estate
Brighton BR4 7HD

Date:

We have received a request for credit from Haven Engineering Ltd who have quoted yourselves as a referee. We would be grateful if you could answer the following questions and return in the stamped addressed envelope enclosed.

How long has the customer been trading with you?	......3.... years ....4.....mths
Your credit terms with customer per month	£ 10,000
Period of credit granted	.....30 days.............................
Payment record	Prompt/occasionally late/slow
Have you ever suspended credit to the customer?	Yes/No
If yes – when and for how long?	....
	....
Any other relevant information	....

....

Thank you for your assistance.

Yours faithfully

Tom Hunt
Credit controller

SC FUEL AND GLASS
CRAWLEY RD
CRAWLEY
CR7 JN9
Tel: 01453 732166 Fax: 01453 732177

Credit controller
Harvard Group Ltd
24/26 Fenwick Way
Dorchester DO3 6HD

Date:

We have received a request for credit from Haven Engineering Ltd who have quoted yourselves as a referee. We would be grateful if you could answer the following questions and return in the stamped addressed envelope enclosed.

How long has the customer
been trading with you?   ......5...   years ....8.....mths

Your credit terms with customer per month   £ 10,000

Period of credit granted   .....30 days...........................

Payment record   Prompt/occasionally late/slow

Have you ever suspended
credit to the customer?   Yes/No

If yes – when and for how long?   ....20X6 for six months...........
                                          ....

Any other relevant information   ....
....
Thank you for your assistance.

Yours faithfully

Tom Hunt
Credit controller

Tom Hunt has also received summarised financial accounts for Haven Engineering Ltd for the three years ending 31 December 20X6, 20X7 and 20X8.

Summarised income statements (profit and loss accounts)

	Year ending 31 December		
	20X6	20X7	20X8
	£'000	£'000	£'000
Revenue (turnover)	3,150	3,220	3,330
Cost of sales	(2,048)	(2,061)	(2,115)
Gross profit	1,102	1,159	1,215
Operating expenses	(645)	(676)	(732)
Operating profit	457	483	483
Interest payable	(95)	(100)	(120)
Profit before tax	362	383	363
Tax	(91)	(96)	(91)
Profit after tax	271	287	272

Summarised statements of financial position (balance sheets)

	As at 31 December		
	20X6	20X7	20X8
	£'000	£'000	£'000
Non-current (fixed) assets	3,339	3,727	4,112
Current assets			
Inventory (stock)	292	328	353
Receivables (debtors)	639	670	684
Cash at bank	2	2	2
	933	1,000	1,039
Current liabilities			
Trade payables (creditors)	494	474	463
Other liabilities	158	146	109
	652	620	572
Net current assets	281	380	467
Total assets less current liabilities	3,620	4,107	4,579
Long term loans	1,600	1,800	2,000
	2,020	2,307	2,579
Ordinary share capital	1,000	1,000	1,000
Retained earnings	1,020	1,307	1,579
	2,020	2,307	2,579

As credit controller Tom Hunt must now assess the information available regarding Haven Engineering Ltd.

Bank reference

The bank reference is not the most positive that might have been given and indicates that consideration should be given, in particular, to the liquidity and profitability of the company.

Trade references

Both trade references indicate that Haven Engineering Ltd is a slow payer and again consideration should be given to information in the financial statements to try to determine whether this is due to liquidity problems, general inefficiency or a determined policy of the company.

Credit was suspended by Harvard Group Ltd in 20X6 for six months, although presumably not since. Finally, it must be noted that both referees only have a credit limit with Haven Engineering Ltd of £10,000 compared with the £15,000 of credit being requested by the company.

Financial statement analysis

	20X6	20X7	20X8
Financial ratios:			
Profitability			
Gross profit margin	35%	36%	36.5%
Net profit margin	14.5%	15%	14.5%
Return on capital employed	12.6%	11.8%	10.5%
Asset turnover	0.87	0.78	0.73
Liquidity			
Current ratio	1.43:1	1.61:1	1.82:1
Quick ratio	0.98:1	1.08:1	1.20:1
Inventory (stock) turnover	52 days	58 days	61 days
Receivables' (debtors') turnover	74 days	76 days	75 days
Payables' (creditors') turnover	88 days	84 days	80 days
Gearing			
Gearing ratio	44%	44%	44%
Interest cover	4.8 times	4.8 times	4.0 times

From the analysis of the financial ratios a number of points can be made about Haven Engineering Ltd.

Profitability

In terms of profitability, the gross profit margin has increased in each of the three years, although the net profit margin is fairly constant. Return on capital employed has fallen over the three years due to the decrease in net asset turnover. There has clearly been large investment in non-current (fixed) assets over the period and as yet this does not appear to have led to largely increased turnover or profits.

Liquidity

The current ratio could be said to be rather low however it has been increasing in each of the three years, and the quick ratio appears healthy and is also improving. The inventory (stock) turnover period is quite high and has increased by nine days over the period, consequently there is considerable capital tied up in the inventory holdings.

Perhaps of more concern are the receivables' (debtors') and payables' (creditors') turnover periods. Receivables' turnover has remained fairly constant but, at around 75 days, is a long time. This might account for the length of time that Haven Engineering Ltd takes to pay its own suppliers which, although improving, still stands at 80 days, which is 50 days longer than SC's credit terms of 30 days.

Gearing

Although there have been small increases annually in the amount of long-term loans, the gearing level has remained constant at 44%. Interest cover is also healthy at four times or over.

Conclusion

The evidence received from the bank reference, trade references and the financial statements would indicate a problem with Haven Engineering regarding the period of time which they take before paying their suppliers. The company appears to be profitable and despite the length of time their own customers take to pay, there would not appear to be too serious a liquidity problem. Therefore the late paying of suppliers could be a deliberate policy.

It is recommended that only £10,000 of credit is initially granted to Haven Engineering Ltd with an agreement that payment is to be strictly within 30 days of the invoice date. This period of credit should perhaps be limited to a six-month period during which the receipts from Haven Engineering Ltd should be monitored closely. Haven Engineering Ltd should be made aware that if payments are not received promptly, credit facilities will be withdrawn and only cash trading will be available.

Task 5

You are the credit controller for a company. You have issued a standard request for bank and trade references in connection with a potential new customer and received the replies set out below.

The potential customer, Conrad Ltd, wishes to trade on credit with your company and has asked for a credit limit of £8,000 with payment terms of payment within 45 days of the invoice date.

What, if any, conclusions could you draw from the references?

Bank reference: Conrad Ltd

Supplied by Bourne Bank

"The customer's credit for £8,000 is considered good for your purposes."

Trade reference: Conrad Ltd

Supplied by XYZ Ltd

How long has the customer been trading
with you?   6 mths

Your credit terms with customer per month   £ 5,000

Period of credit granted   .... 30 days...............

Payment record   Prompt/occasionally late/slow

Have you ever suspended credit
to the customer?   Yes/No

If yes – when and for how long?..

Any other relevant information ....

....

Sale of goods and supply of services

So far in this chapter we have considered businesses which supply goods to other parties. However some businesses such as accountants, advertising agencies etc provide a service rather than provide goods. Such services may still be provided on credit and similar checks need to be made on the customer to ensure that they are creditworthy.

However the provision of services can be different in nature as they can sometimes be much longer term than the supply of goods. For example a supplier of IT services to a business may be on a five year contract with the business whereby invoices are sent to the business every six months. In these circumstances clearly the long-term viability of the customer is of utmost importance and must be considered when looking at the information available about the customer.

CREDIT SCORING

CREDIT SCORING is a method of assessing the creditworthiness of an individual or organisation using statistical analysis and is used by organisations such as banks, utility companies, insurance companies and landlords to assess the ability of an individual or organisation to repay any loans or pay for services or goods.

Credit reference agencies, which we discussed earlier in this chapter, buy information regarding shareholders, directors, and statutory accounts from official sources like Companies House and the Registry Trust (the body that collects and stores County Court Judgment data). They supplement this information with trade directory data and they use their own techniques to collect proprietary information, such as interviewing companies by phone or gathering information on businesses by sending questionnaires. In the UK, the activities of credit reference agencies are governed by UK legislation, including the Data Protection Act 1998.

All the information is entered into a scoring system, and a credit score is then calculated by weighting the information. Using the credit score, lenders can predict with some accuracy how likely the borrower is to repay a debt and make payments on time.

Leading credit reference agencies use data from multiple sources to create a comprehensive, weighted score. Typically they will consider:

- Financials – profitability, liquidity/solvency, gearing, any late filing of accounts or other statutory documents

- Business details – age, size, industry, number of employees

- Publicly available data – County Court Judgments, mortgages and charges

- Payment record – payment trends, volatility, % of debts paid promptly or beyond terms

- Owners – number, experience, track record

- Economic index – risk and expectations relating to the specific industry under different economic conditions

A business that can demonstrate timely payment of its obligations, assets which easily outweigh its liabilities, a large amount of available credit and one that is not too highly geared will be deemed low risk.

Late payments and high gearing will damage the score and any insolvency/bankruptcy, judgments and foreclosure will almost certainly guarantee a failing grade.

A business may use its own credit rating system to assess the credit status of new and existing customers based on analysis of its financial statements, where an aggregate score is calculated from a number of key ratios and this is then used to provide a risk assessment of the customer.

HOW IT WORKS

In the AAT sample assessment the following credit scoring system was provided:

The credit rating (scoring) system table below is used to assess the risk of default by calculating key indicators (ratios), comparing them to the table and calculating an aggregate score.

Credit rating (scoring) system	Score
Operating profit margin	
Losses	–5
Less than 5%	0
5% and above but less than 10%	5
10% and above but less than 20%	10
More than 20%	20
Interest cover	
No cover	–30
Less than 1	–20
More than 1 but less than 2	–10
More than 2 but less than 4	0
More than 4	10
Liquidity ratio	
Less than 1	–20
Between 1 and 1.25	–10
Between 1.25 and 1.5	0
Above 1.5	10

Credit rating (scoring) system	Score
Gearing (total debt/(total debt plus equity))	
Less than 25%	20
25% and above but less than 50%	10
More than 50% less than 65%	0
Between 65% and 75%	−20
Between 75% and 80%	−40
Above 80%	−100
Risk	**Aggregate score**
Very low risk	Between 60 and 21
Low risk	Between 20 and 1
Medium risk	Between 0 and −24
High risk	Between −25 and −50
Very high risk	Above −50

COMMUNICATION OF CREDIT ASSESSMENT DECISION

Once a decision has been taken to grant credit to a customer, then the precise details of the credit limit and all terms and conditions of trading and payment must be communicated to the new customer in writing. Before this is done the credit limit must be set for the customer. When determining this, communication with the sales department will be useful to establish the expected level of orders from this customer. For example, if the sales department expects the customer to order £4,000 of goods per week and the credit terms are 30 days then a credit limit of, say, £10,000 would seriously limit the sales to this customer.

HOW IT WORKS

It has been agreed at SC Fuel and Glass that Haven Engineering Ltd should be offered a trial period of credit of six months due to their apparently slow supplier payment policy. During this time all receipts will be carefully monitored and if payment is not received within 30 days of the invoice date then the credit facility will be withdrawn.

Tom Hunt has now drafted the letter that will be sent to Haven Engineering Ltd agreeing these terms and conditions.

SC FUEL AND GLASS
CRAWLEY RD
CRAWLEY
CR7 JN9
Tel: 01453 732166 Fax: 01453 732177

Finance Director
Haven Engineering Ltd
Fairstop Park
Havant HV4 7BN

Date:

Dear Sir

Re: Request for credit facilities

Thank you for your enquiry regarding the provision of credit facilities to yourselves of £15,000 on 30-day terms. We have taken up your bank and trade references and examined your last three years of financial statements.

Although your references are satisfactory, we have some concerns about your supplier payment policy which appears to be excessively long. Although your profitability and liquidity generally appear sound we would not normally extend credit on the type of time-scale on which you appear to pay your suppliers.

However due to your bank and trade references we are happy to offer you a credit facility for six months at the end of which time the movement on your account will be reviewed and the position re-assessed. The credit limit that we can offer you would initially be £10,000 and the payment terms are strictly 30 days from the invoice date.

Thank you for your interest in our company and we look forward to trading with you on the basis set out above.

Yours faithfully

Tom Hunt
Credit controller

Opening a new customer account

Once a decision has been made to grant credit to a customer then a file and an account in the receivables (debtors) ledger must be set up. For this to take place the following information will be required:

- The business name of the customer
- The contact name and title within the customer's business
- Business address and telephone number
- The credit limit agreed upon
- The payment terms agreed
- Any other terms such as settlement discounts offered (see Chapter 4 of this Text)

REFUSAL OF CREDIT

In many cases once the credit controller has carried out checks on a new potential customer such as bank references, trade references, credit agency reports and analysis of financial statements then a decision will be made to grant the customer credit, the terms of payment will be communicated to the new customer and an account set up in the receivables (debtors) ledger.

However, in some cases, the credit controller may decide that it is not possible to trade with a new potential customer on credit terms.

Reasons for refusal of credit

Refusing to grant credit to a new customer is a big decision for the credit controller, as the business will not wish to lose this potential customer's business but the credit controller will have taken a view that the risk of non-payment is too high for credit terms to be granted.

Refusal of credit does not necessarily mean that the potential customer's business is bad or is likely not to survive; it simply means that on the evidence available to the credit controller, the chance of non-payment is too high for the company to take the risk.

There are a variety of reasons why a decision might be made not to grant credit to a new customer and could include the following:

- A non-committal or poor bank reference

- Poor trade references

- Concerns about the validity of any trade references submitted

- Adverse press comment about the potential customer

- Poor credit agency report

- Information from a member of the business's credit circle

- Indications of business weakness from analysis of the financial statements

- Lack of historical financial statements available due to being a recently started company

The credit controller will consider all of the evidence available about a potential customer and the reason for the refusal of credit may be due to a single factor noted above or a combination of factors.

Communication of refusal of credit

If credit is not to be granted to a potential customer then this must be communicated in a tactful and diplomatic manner. The reasons for the refusal of credit must be politely explained and any future actions required from the potential customer should also be made quite clear. The credit controller, while not wishing to grant credit to the customer at the current time, will also not necessarily want to lose their potential business.

Trading on cash terms

In almost all cases where credit is to be refused to a potential customer the company should make it quite clear that they would be happy to trade with the customer on cash terms. This may be acceptable to the customer, even if it is not the desired outcome, and their business will not be lost.

Future re-assessment of creditworthiness

In some situations, although the granting of credit to the new customer has currently been refused, it may be that the credit controller wishes to encourage the customer to apply for credit terms in the future. For example, with a newly formed company, there may be little external information available on which the credit controller can rely at the present time but if financial statements and references can be provided in the future then the decision as to whether or not to trade on credit terms can be re-assessed.

Communication method

In most cases it is usually expedient to communicate the reasons for the refusal of credit initially in a letter. In the letter the credit controller may suggest that a telephone call may be appropriate in order to discuss the matter and any future actions that may be necessary.

HOW IT WORKS

In the last week Tom Hunt has also been assessing requests for credit from two other potential new customers.

Glowform Ltd has requested to trade with the fuel division on credit and would like a £5,000 credit limit and 60 days' credit. Tom requested two trade references, a bank reference and financial statements for the last three years. Glowform Ltd has provided a bank reference which states that the "the company appears to be well constituted but we cannot necessarily speak for your figures due to the length of time that the company has been in operation." The company has also provided one trade reference which is satisfactory from a company which allows Glowform Ltd £3,000 of credit on 30-day terms. However Glowform Ltd has only been in operation for just over a year and has, as yet, not been able to provide any financial statements.

Joseph Partners has requested 30 days of credit and a credit limit of £6,000. It has provided its statement of financial position (balance sheet) at its last year end which was four months ago, and the income statement (profit and loss account) for the year to that date. The financial statements indicate fairly low levels of profitability but there is nothing to compare the figures to. The bank reference is satisfactory but of the two trade references, one has only been trading with Joseph Partners for two months.

The two letters which Tom Hunt has drafted to these businesses are shown below.

SC FUEL AND GLASS
CRAWLEY RD
CRAWLEY
CR7 JN9
Tel: 01453 732166 Fax: 01453 732177

Finance Director
Glowform Ltd

Date:

Dear Sir

Re: Request for credit facilities

Thank you for your enquiry regarding the provision of credit facilities of £5,000 of credit on 60-day terms. We have taken up your trade and bank references of which you kindly sent details.

We have some concerns about offering credit at this early stage of your business as there are as yet no financial statements for your business that we can examine. Therefore at this stage I am unable to confirm that we can provide you with credit facilities immediately.

We would, of course, be delighted to trade with you on cash terms until we have had an opportunity to examine your first year's trading figures. Therefore please send us a copy of your first year financial statements when they are available and in the meantime contact us if you would like to start trading on a cash basis.

Thank you for your interest in our company.

Yours faithfully

Tom Hunt
Credit controller

SC FUEL AND GLASS
CRAWLEY RD
CRAWLEY
CR7 JN9
Tel: 01453 732166 Fax: 01453 732177

Finance Partner
Joseph Partners

Date:

Dear Sir

Re: Request for credit facilities

Thank you for your enquiry regarding the provision of credit facilities of £6,000 on 30-day terms. We have taken up your trade references and examined your latest set of financial statements.

We have some concerns about your level of profitability and would like the opportunity to examine your statements of financial position (balance sheets) and income statements (profit and loss accounts) for the two previous years. As one of your trade references has only been trading with you for two months we would also request details of a further supplier that we could contact for a trade reference.

At this stage I am unable to confirm that we can provide you with a credit facility but we will reconsider the situation when we receive your financial statements and additional trade reference.

Thank you for your interest in our company and in the meantime we would, of course, be delighted to trade with you on a cash terms basis.

Yours faithfully

Tom Hunt
Credit controller

Task 6

What potential reasons could there be for not agreeing to trade on credit with a new customer?

CHAPTER OVERVIEW

- When evaluating a customer's credit status the concerns will be whether the customer will pay within the stated credit terms and that their business will remain solvent.

- When either a potential new customer requests credit or an existing customer requests an increase in credit limit, the credit controller will make use of internal and external information in order to determine whether or not the request should be granted.

- External sources of information are most commonly a bank reference and two trade references.

- In some cases a credit controller will use the services of a credit reference agency for information about a potential customer and a possible credit rating or rather more informally from any credit circle that they may belong to.

- Other sources of external information are Companies House records, official publications and the internet.

- It may also be possible for the potential customer to provide internal management accounts.

- When considering requests from existing customers it is likely that staff within the business will have internal information about the customer and may possibly have made visits to the customer's premises.

- The most common form of internal analysis of both existing and potential new customers is financial ratio analysis of their financial accounts, preferably for the last three years or more.

- Once all of the relevant information has been gathered about a customer then a decision must be made as to whether or not to grant them credit – in many cases the information may be conflicting with some sources suggesting that credit should be granted and other sources not proving so favourable.

- Credit scoring is a method used by organisations such as banks and utility companies to assess the creditworthiness of an individual or organisation.

- Once a decision has been made as to whether or not to grant credit to a customer, this decision must be communicated to the customer, normally in writing.

- Where credit is to be granted to a new customer, the details of the credit limit and terms of payment must be made quite clear and a new account for that customer must be opened within the receivables (debtors) ledger.

- In some cases it may be decided to refuse credit to a customer in which case this must be communicated in a tactful and diplomatic manner.

- In some cases a customer may be offered a chance for future re-assessment of their credit status and in the meantime an offer for trading on cash terms would be made.

Keywords

Bank reference – a bank's opinion of its customer's business position and credit status

Trade reference – a reference from one of a business's current suppliers regarding their payment record

Credit application form – a form sent to a prospective new customer asking for details including bank and trade reference details

Credit reference agency – commercial organisation providing background information and credit status information about companies and individuals

Credit circles – groups of companies who are normally competitors who can provide mutual information on current and prospective customers and their credit records

Gross profit margin – measure of the profit from trading activities compared with revenue

Net profit margin – measure of the overall profit compared with revenue

Return on capital employed – measure of the overall profit compared with total capital employed

Capital employed – share capital, reserves and long-term debt; also alternatively measured as the net asset total of the business

Net asset turnover – measure of the amount of revenue compared with total capital employed

Current ratio – current assets as a ratio to current liabilities

Quick/acid test ratio – current assets minus inventory (stock) as a ratio to current liabilities

Inventory (stock) turnover – the average number of days which inventory is held for

Receivables' (debtors') turnover – the average number of days before receivables pay the amounts owed

Payables' (creditors') turnover – the average number of days credit taken from trade payables

Working capital cycle – inventory (stock) turnover days + receivables' (debtors') turnover days – payables' (creditors') turnover days

Gearing ratio – the total long-term debt capital as a percentage of the total capital employed

Interest cover – the number of times the annual interest payment is covered by profits earned

EBITDA – earnings before interest and tax, depreciation and amortisation

Credit scoring – a method of assessing the creditworthiness of an individual or organisation, which is performed by credit reference agencies using statistical analysis

TEST YOUR LEARNING

Test 1

You are the credit controller for AKA Ltd and you are considering a request from Kelvin & Sons who wish to trade on credit with your company. You are considering offering them a credit limit of £10,000 with payment terms of payment within 30 days of the invoice date.

You have written to Kelvin & Sons' bank, Southern Bank, asking for a reference having specified that you are considering a credit limit of £10,000. The bank's reply is given below.

"Should prove good for your figures"

What, if any, conclusions can you draw from the bank reference?

A   Credit should be granted.

B   Credit should not be granted.

C   Credit should be granted if further information is positive.

D   No conclusion can be drawn.

Test 2

You are the credit controller for a company and you are considering a request from Caterham Ltd who wish to trade on credit with your company. Caterham Ltd asked for a credit limit of £15,000 with payment terms of payment within 30 days of the invoice date. You have a standard form for trade references and Caterham Ltd has provided you with the name and address of another supplier of theirs, SK Traders, to whom you have sent the standard trade reference form. The reply you receive is given below.

Trade reference

We have received a request for credit from Caterham Ltd who have quoted yourselves as a referee. We would be grateful if you could answer the following questions and return in the stamped addressed envelope enclosed.

How long has the customer been trading
with you?   ..4.. years . 2... mths

Your credit terms with customer per month   £ 8,000

Period of credit granted   .... 30 days..............

Payment record   Prompt/occasionally late/slow

Have you ever suspended credit
to the customer?   Yes/No

If yes – when and for how long?..

Any other relevant information ....

....

Thank you for your assistance.

What, if any, conclusions could you draw from the trade reference?

Test 3

What services does a credit reference agency typically provide?

Test 4

Which of the following information could be provided by Companies House
about a company that was requesting credit from your business?

A   Management accounts

B   Directors' contracts

C   Annual financial statements

D   Loan agreements

Test 5

You are the credit controller for a business and you have been approached by Franklin Ltd who wish to place an order with your business and wish to trade on credit. It would like a credit limit of £5,000 per month. Franklin Ltd has provided you with its last two years' income statements (profit and loss accounts) and statements of financial position (balance sheets).

Income statements for the year ended 31 March

	20X9	20X8
	£'000	£'000
Revenue (turnover)	1,000	940
Cost of sales	(780)	(740)
Gross profit	220	200
Operating expenses	(100)	(90)
Operating profit	120	110
Interest payable	(30)	(20)
Profit before tax	90	90
Taxation	(23)	(23)
Profit after tax	67	67

Statements of financial position at 31 March

	20X9	20X8
	£'000	£'000
Non-current (fixed) assets	1,335	1,199
Current assets		
Inventory (stock)	110	90
Receivables (debtors)	140	150
	250	240
Current liabilities		
Trade payables (creditors)	160	161
Bank overdraft	300	200
	460	361
Net assets	1,125	1,078
Share capital	800	800
Retained earnings	325	278
	1,125	1,078

Complete the table below by calculating the ratios given.

	20X9	20X8
Gross profit margin		
Net profit margin		
Return on capital employed		
Current ratio		
Quick ratio		
Payables' (creditors') payment period		
Interest cover		

Test 6

You are the credit manager for Acorn Enterprises and your name is Jo Wilkie. You have been assessing the financial statements for Little Partners who have requested £8,000 of credit on 60-day terms. You also have received a satisfactory bank reference and trade references.

Your analysis of the 20X7 and 20X8 financial statements show the following picture:

	20X8	20X7
Gross profit margin	30%	28%
Net profit margin	4%	3%
Interest cover	1.5 times	0.9 times
Current ratio	1.3 times	0.8 times

You are to draft a suitable letter to Little Partners dealing with their request for credit facilities.

Test 7

You are the credit controller for a business and you received a request from Dawn Ltd for credit of £5,000 from your company on a 30-day basis. Two trade references have been provided but no bank reference. You have also been provided with the last set of published financial statements which include the previous year's comparative figures. The trade references appeared satisfactory although one is from Johannesson Partners and it has been noted that the managing director of Dawn Ltd is Mr F Johannesson. Analysis of the financial statements has indicated a decrease in profitability during the last year, a high level of gearing and low liquidity ratios.

Draft a letter to the finance director of Dawn Ltd on the basis that credit is to be currently refused but may be extended once the most recent financial statements have been examined.

chapter 3:
LEGISLATION AND
CREDIT CONTROL

— chapter coverage 📖 —

There are a number of ways in which legislation impacts upon credit control. The sale of goods and services is a contract and therefore the fundamentals of contract law must be understood. Therefore before we look at methods of managing the supply of credit and collecting debts from customers, we spend this chapter considering the impact of legislation on this area.

The topics covered are:

✍ Contract law

✍ Agreement

✍ Value

✍ Intention to create legal relations

✍ Breach of contract

✍ Bankruptcy and insolvency

✍ Other legislation

✍ Data protection

CONTRACT LAW

The relationship between a seller of goods and a buyer of goods is a contract and therefore in this section we must consider the basics of contract law.

What is a contract?

A CONTRACT is a legally binding agreement enforceable in a court of law.

As an individual you will enter into contracts every day – when you buy goods in a shop, when you place an order for goods over the telephone, when you employ a plumber to fix a leak. These contracts are usually verbal but contracts can also be in writing, for example, if you take out a loan from your bank there will be a written contract.

During your working hours you will also be part of the process of contracts being made between your organisation and its customers and suppliers.

The importance of contract law

The importance of contract law is that if a contract is validly made between two parties then if one party does not satisfactorily carry out their side of the agreement, the other party can take the defaulting party to court for BREACH OF CONTRACT (see later in this chapter).

How is a contract formed?

For a contract to be formed and to be valid there must be three main elements:

Agreement + Value + Intention to create legal relations = Contract

AGREEMENT

In legal terms, for there to be a valid agreement there must be a valid OFFER and a valid acceptance of that offer.

There will be two parties to a contract – the OFFEROR and the OFFEREE. The offeror is the person making the offer and the offeree is the person to whom the offer is made. The offer is an expression of willingness to contract on a specific set of terms and may be verbal or it may be in writing.

HOW IT WORKS

The glass division of SC Fuel and Glass has received a purchase enquiry from a large building contractor concerning the purchase of 1,000 sealed glazed units. For such a large order the glass division is prepared to reduce the price charged from the normal price of £80 to £78 per unit and has sent out a purchase quotation stating this price for the 1,000 units.

This will become a valid offer from SC Fuel and Glass to the building contractor when the building contractor receives the purchase quotation in the post. Obviously, it is important that the price quoted is correct as, if not, the building contractor could legally require SC to sell the units to them at the price quoted.

Remember also that an offer can be made verbally, so if quoting a price to a customer over the telephone, ensure that it is the correct price as it will be a valid offer.

An invitation to treat

Care must be taken to distinguish between an offer and an INVITATION TO TREAT. An invitation to treat is an invitation by the seller of goods for the buyer to make an offer to buy them at that price. Examples of invitations to treat are advertisements for goods, catalogues and price tickets displayed on goods.

HOW IT WORKS

The glass division of SC Fuel and Glass issue a catalogue to potential and existing customers twice a year showing the different types of double-glazed units available and their prices. This is an invitation to treat and not an offer, therefore SC is not necessarily tied to the prices quoted in the catalogue. If a customer enquires about purchasing goods from the catalogue then they are making an offer to buy the goods at the catalogue price. It is then up to SC to decide whether or not to accept this offer by selling to the customer at the published price or changing the price if circumstances have changed.

Task 1

John is in a car showroom and sees a price ticket on a car of £2,395. He offers to buy the car at this price but is informed by the salesman that there was an error on the price ticket which should have read £12,395.

Can John insist on buying the car at £2,395? Explain the reason for your answer.

Duration of an offer

If an offer is made then it does not have to remain in place indefinitely. There are a number of ways in which an offer can be brought to an end:

- If there is a set time period for an offer then the offer will lapse at the end of that time period. If there is no express time period set then the offer will lapse after a reasonable period of time.

- An offer can be revoked by the offeror at any point in time before it has been accepted – REVOCATION of an offer means that the offer is cancelled.
- An offer comes to an end if it is rejected. Care must be taken here as rejection need not only be by the offeree specifically saying no to the offer. An offer is also rejected by a COUNTER-OFFER. For example, if an offer is made to sell an item for £1,000 and the offeree replies to say that he will buy it at a price of £900 this is rejection of the original offer to sell.
- The offer also comes to an end when a valid ACCEPTANCE is made.

Acceptance of an offer

The ACCEPTANCE of an offer must be an absolute and unqualified acceptance.

- Acceptance can be made verbally or in writing.
- If an offer requires a particular form of acceptance (verbal, in writing, by fax) then this is the form in which the acceptance must be made.
- The acceptance must be unqualified – if any additional conditions or terms are included in an acceptance then this takes the form of a counter-offer which rejects the original offer.

HOW IT WORKS

When SC sent the purchase quotation to the building contractor for the 1,000 sealed double-glazed units for £78 each this was an offer. If the building contractor replies that it will buy the units at this price but they must be delivered tomorrow then this is a counter-offer which rejects SC's original offer. It is then up to SC to determine whether or not to accept this new counter-offer and sell the units to the building contractor under these terms.

VALUE

The second required element of a contract is that of there being some value. The basis of contract law is that we are dealing with a bargain of some sort, not just a promise by one of the parties to a contract to do something.

What is required for there to be a valid contract is known in legal terms as CONSIDERATION. Consideration can be thought of as something given, promised or done in exchange for the action of the other party.

In terms of business transactions the consideration given for a sale of goods is either the money paid now or the promise by a receivable (debtor) to pay at a later date.

INTENTION TO CREATE LEGAL RELATIONS

Finally, for a contract to be valid there must be an intention to create legal relations.

Remember that a contract is a legally binding agreement which means that if one party does not fully play their part in the contract, the other party can take them to court for breach of contract. However, many agreements that are made are never intended to be legally binding.

In general terms, agreements with friends and family of a social nature are presumed not to have any intention to create legal relations.

In contrast, business agreements are presumed to be intended to create legal relations and therefore can be enforced by the law.

Defective contracts

There are some situations in which a contract will only have limited legal effect or even no legal effect at all.

A void contract is not a contract at all. The parties are not bound by it and if they transfer property under it, they can sometimes recover their goods even from a third party. This normally comes about due to some form of common mistake on a fundamental issue of the contract.

A voidable contract is a contract which one party may set aside. Property transferred before avoidance is usually irrecoverable from a third party. Such contracts may be with minors or contracts induced by misrepresentation, duress or undue influence.

An unenforceable contract is a valid contract and property transferred under it cannot be recovered even from the other party to the contract. But if either party refuses to perform or to complete their part of the performance of the contract, the other party cannot compel them to do so. A contract is usually unenforceable when the required evidence of its terms, for example, written evidence of a contract relating to land, is not available.

BREACH OF CONTRACT

We mentioned earlier in this chapter that one party to a contract can take the other to court for BREACH OF CONTRACT. Breach of contract is where one party to the contract does not fulfil his part of the agreement.

HOW IT WORKS

If SC agrees to supply the 1,000 glazed units to the building contractor tomorrow and then fails to do so, SC would be in breach of contract. It would be possible for the building contractor to take SC to court to claim damages for any losses due to this breach of contract.

Equally, on supply of the units to the building contractor on time, SC would expect the building contractor to pay for the goods within the stated credit period. If the building contractor does not pay it will be in breach of contract and can, in turn, be taken to court in order for payment to be made.

Terms in a contract

In most contracts there are certain terms that must be fulfilled in order for the contract to be carried out. If the terms of a contract are not fulfilled then one party will be in breach of contract. Legally, different terms of a contract have different effects.

EXPRESS TERMS are terms that are specifically stated in the contract and are binding on both parties.

CONDITIONS are terms that are fundamental to the contract and if they are broken then the party breaking them will be in breach of contract and can be sued for damages. The injured party can regard the contract as ended.

WARRANTIES are less important terms in a contract. If any of these are not fulfilled then there is breach of contract but the contract remains in force. The injured party can still claim damages from the court for any loss suffered, but he cannot treat the contract as terminated.

IMPLIED TERMS are terms of a contract which are not specifically stated but are implied in such a contract either by trade custom or by the law.

Task 2

What is meant by consideration within contract law?

A   The payment of the contract price

B   The necessary agreement to the contract terms

C   The valid acceptance of an offer

D   The promise to exchange value

Remedies for breach of contract

A breach of contract arises where one party to the contract does not carry out their side of the bargain, such as a credit customer who does not pay. There are a number of remedies available to the injured party for breach of contract.

These include:

- Action for the price – a court action to recover the agreed price of the goods/services

- Monetary damages – compensation for loss

- Termination – one party refusing to carry on with the contract

- Specific performance – a court order that one of the parties must fulfil their obligations

- *Quantum meruit* – payment ordered for the part of the contract performed

- Injunction – one party to the contract being ordered by the court not to do something

In terms of a credit customer not having paid for goods or services provided, the most appropriate remedy would normally be an action for the price.

Bringing a dispute to court

If it is decided that the only course of action to recover money owed by a credit customer is that of legal action, then the first step is to instruct a solicitor. The solicitor will require details of the goods or services provided, the date the liability arose, the exact name and trading status of the customer, any background information such as disputes in the past and a copy of any invoices that are unpaid.

In some instances, the threat of legal action will be enough and even after the solicitor has been involved there can be a negotiated settlement between the business and their customer, as the customer may not want to run the risk of going to court and any costs that might be incurred. However, in other situations the case will be taken to court.

Which court?

If the claim is for less than £5,000 then the case will be made in the small claims division of the County Court, under what is known as the small claims track. Any other claims for between £5,000 and £25,000 will normally be dealt with in the County Court under the fast track procedure, whereby the case is heard speedily. Complex claims involving amounts greater than £25,000 will be heard under the multi-track procedure, in either the County Court or the High Court, depending on the complexity of the case.

Procedure

Once the appropriate court has received all of the paperwork for the claim it will issue a summons to the customer requiring an acknowledgement of service of the summons. If the customer does not reply then the judgement will go against him.

The customer may admit the claim and perhaps offer to pay by instalments. If the business does not accept this then the court will determine a suitable method of paying off the debt.

Task 3

An action is to be brought against a customer for unpaid amounts of £10,000.

In which court would this action normally be brought?

A   County Court

B   Small Claims Court

C   High Court

D   Employment Tribunal

Methods of receiving payment under a court order

Once there has been a court order that the money due must be paid there are a number of methods of achieving this:

- Attachment of earnings order – the business will be paid the amount owing directly by the customer's employer as a certain amount is deducted from their weekly/monthly pay. However this is only viable for a customer who is an individual and is in stable, consistent work.

- Third-party debt order (garnishee order) – this allows the business to be paid directly by a third party who owes the business's customer money.

- Warrant of execution – a court bailiff seizes and sells the customer's goods on behalf of the business.

- Administrative order – the customer makes regular, agreed payments into court to pay off the debt.

- Receiver – a receiver is appointed to receive money that will be owing to the customer, eg rents.

- Charge – a legal charge is taken on property or financial assets, so the supplier is paid when the assets are sold.

- Bankruptcy notice – see next section.

- Liquidation – see next section.

HOW IT WORKS

SC Fuel and Glass is owed £2,800 by one of its hauliers, Terence Frame & Sons. The claim was taken to the Small Claims Court and Terence Frame & Sons were ordered to pay the full amount due. This was done by a garnishee order, whereby a third party, Cranford Garages Ltd who owed Terence Frame & Sons £4,000 themselves paid over an amount of £2,800 to SC Fuel and Glass.

BANKRUPTCY AND INSOLVENCY

BANKRUPTCY arises where an individual cannot pay their debts and is declared bankrupt and INSOLVENCY is where a company cannot pay their debts as they fall due.

When assessing bad debts, if an individual customer is bankrupt or a corporate customer is insolvent, then the business may receive little or nothing of the amount due. It is important to be aware of bankruptcy and insolvency legal issues as the use of bankruptcy or insolvency legislation may become the only course available for a business in order to receive payment or at least part-payment of an amount due.

Petition for bankruptcy

If a receivable (debtor) owes an amount of at least £750 a STATUTORY DEMAND can be issued for payment of the amount due within a certain period of time. This may result in the customer offering a settlement. If, however, there is no settlement offer from the customer a petition for bankruptcy will be received from the court.

Consequences of a petition for bankruptcy

The consequences of a petition for bankruptcy against a receivable are:

- If the customer pays money to any other suppliers or disposes of any property then these transactions are void.

- Any other legal proceedings relating to the customer's property or debts are suspended.

- An interim receiver is appointed to protect the estate.

Consequences of a bankruptcy order

The consequences of a bankruptcy order are:

- The official receiver takes control of the assets of the business.

- A statement of the assets and liabilities is drawn up – this is known as a STATEMENT OF AFFAIRS.

- The receiver summons a meeting of creditors of the individual within 12 weeks of the bankruptcy order.

- The creditors of the individual appoint a trustee in bankruptcy.

- The assets of the business are realised and distribution is made to the various creditors.

- The creditor who presented the petition does not gain any priority for payment over other creditors.

Order of distribution of assets

The assets of the bankrupt will be distributed in the following order:

- Secured creditors

- Bankruptcy costs

- Preferential creditors such as employees, pension schemes, HM Revenue & Customs

- Unsecured creditors such as trade payables (creditors)

- The bankrupt's spouse

- The bankrupt

As an unsecured trade payable a business with debts due from a bankrupt should submit a written claim to the trustee detailing how the debt is made up. This may also need to be substantiated with documentary evidence. As the payment of unsecured creditors comes after many other payments, the supplier may receive little or nothing towards the amount owed. Often this is in the form of a "dividend" so, for example, if a bankrupt owed £100,000 to creditors but has only £20,000 left after other payments have been made, then a trade payable will only receive 20 pence for every pound that he is owed.

Task 4

What is the difference between bankruptcy and insolvency?

Insolvency

The process of insolvency for a company that cannot pay its debts as they fall due is similar to that of a bankrupt individual. There are two main options for companies:

- Liquidation
- Administration

Liquidation

In a liquidation the company is dissolved and the assets are realised with debts being paid from the proceeds and any excess being returned to the shareholders. This process is carried out by a liquidator on behalf of the shareholders and/or creditors. The liquidator's job is simply to ensure that the creditors are paid and once this is done the company can be wound-up. Again, unsecured creditors are a long way down the list of who is paid first, therefore there may be little left in the pot.

Administration

An alternative to a liquidation is that the shareholders, directors or creditors can present a petition to the court for an administration order. The effect of this is that the company continues to operate but an insolvency practitioner (administrator) is put in control of it, with the purpose of trying to save the company from insolvency, as a going concern, or at least achieve a better result than a liquidation.

Retention of title clause

A retention of title clause can be written into agreements with customers. Such a clause states that the buyer does not obtain ownership of the goods unless and until payment is made. Accordingly, if the buyer does go out of business before paying for the goods, the supplier can retrieve them.

> **Task 5**
>
> What is the role of an insolvency practitioner under an administration order?

OTHER LEGISLATION

There are a number of other areas of legislation which are relevant to the subject of granting and managing credit which you should be aware of.

Trade Descriptions Act

The Trade Descriptions Act makes it a criminal offence to declare false or misleading statements about goods being sold or services being provided.

For example, if a business stated that a particular product was now being sold for £24.99 reduced from £49.99 this would be a criminal offence if, in fact, the product had previously been sold at a price of £39.99.

Unfair Contract Terms Act

The purpose of this legislation is to ensure that "unfair terms" cannot be included in contracts normally in the "small print".

Where standard terms are used in a contractual relationship businesses are not entitled to exclude or limit liability arising from their own breach, or change the performance of the contract in the event of a BREACH OF CONTRACT the business,

Indemnity clauses are also regulated by the Unfair Contract Terms Act and a consumer cannot be made to indemnify another party to the contract.

Liability for defective consumer goods cannot be limited or excluded.

The Unfair Contract Terms Act also prohibits the exclusion of terms implied into a contract by the Sale of Goods Act (see below).

Sale of Goods Act

Contracts for the sale of goods are governed by the Sale of Goods Acts 1893 and 1979. The Acts state the following regarding title to the goods:

- Where the goods are ready for delivery (ie for the buyer and/or carrier to take), title to the property passes immediately even if payment is delayed: a sale on credit.

- Goods sold by 'sale or return'. Title only passes when the buyer approves of the goods (eg does not state that he or she rejects them).

Where goods are sold in a shop the Acts state that there are three key necessities for the goods. They must be:

- "Satisfactory quality" – this is the standard of quality that a reasonable person would expect given the description of the goods and their price.

- "Fit for the purpose" – the goods do what they would be expected to do or what the shop claims they can do.

- "As described" – the goods must be what they are described to be – for example an automatic car must have an automatic gearbox.

Late Payment of Commercial Debts (Interest) Act

This legislation was introduced in 1998 and gave small businesses the right to claim interest from large business customers or public sector customers who pay late. The legislation was amended in 2002 so that all businesses, irrespective of size, and public sector bodies now have the statutory right to claim interest from all business and public sector customers on debts incurred under contracts agreed after that date. It is for the supplier to decide whether or not to make a claim for interest.

The statutory interest rate chargeable is the Bank of England base rate plus 8%. This was set so that small businesses could cover late payments by bank borrowings. Interest runs from the day after the credit period if the customer has not paid within the agreed credit period. If there is no agreed credit period, the legislation sets a default credit period of 30 days after which interest can run. The interest can be calculated using the following formula:

Gross debt x (Bank of England base rate + 8%) x (number of days late/365)

Once statutory interest runs on a qualifying debt, the supplier is also entitled under the legislation to claim a fixed sum for compensation as follows:

- For debts less than £1000, the supplier can claim £40.
- For debts between £1000 and £9,999.99, the supplier can claim £70.
- For debts of £10,000 or more, the supplier can claim £100.

Consumer Credit Act

This Act gives additional rights to individuals (rather than companies) who are credit customers of a business. The aim of the Act is to ensure that individuals that become credit customers of a business are fully aware of what they have agreed to.

DATA PROTECTION

Due to the growth in the use of computer technology the DATA PROTECTION ACT was introduced to restrict the use of data held about individuals and the use of personal data. It is likely that your organisation maintains data about credit customers and therefore you need to be aware of the broad outlines of the Act. Be aware that the provisions of the Data Protection Act relate to paper-based systems as well as computer systems.

It is important to realise that the Act relates to personal information data held about individuals not about organisations, so will only be relevant to non-corporate customers or to data about individuals who belong to a customer organisation.

Important definitions from the Act

PERSONAL INFORMATION held about a living individual, not only factual information but also expressions of opinion about that individual.

A DATA SUBJECT is an individual who is the subject of personal data.

A DATA CONTROLLER is a person who holds and processes personal information.

Principles of good practice for data controllers

The Act sets out eight principles of good practice which must be followed by data controllers to ensure that personal data is handled properly. These principles state that personal data must be:

- Fairly and lawfully processed (see below)

- Processed for limited purposes

- Adequate, relevant and not excessive

- Accurate and up-to-date

- Not kept for longer than necessary

- Processed in line with the data subject's rights

- Kept securely

- Not transferred to countries outside the EU unless such data is adequately protected in those countries.

Data subjects' rights under the Act

Data subjects have seven rights under the Data Protection Act.

- **The right to subject access** – this allows people to find out what information is held about them on computer and within some manual records.

- **The right to prevent processing** – anyone can ask a data controller not to process data relating to them that causes substantial unwarranted damage or distress to them or anyone else.

- **The right to prevent processing for direct marketing** – anyone can ask a data controller not to process data relating to them for direct marketing purposes.

- **Rights in relation to automated decision-taking** – individuals have a right to object to decisions made only by automatic means, eg there is no human involvement.

- **The right to compensation** – an individual can claim compensation from a data controller for damage and distress caused by any breach of the Act. Compensation for distress alone can only be claimed in limited circumstances.

- **The right to rectification, blocking, erasure and destruction** – individuals can apply to the courts to order a data controller to rectify, block or destroy personal details if they are inaccurate or contain expression of opinion based on inaccurate data.

- **The right to ask the Commissioner to assess whether the Act has been contravened** – if someone believes their personal information has not been processed in accordance with the Data Protection Act, they can ask the Commissioner to make an assessment. If the Act is found to have been breached and the matter cannot be settled informally, then an enforcement notice may be served on the data controller in question.

Task 6

Which of the following pieces of legislation gives rights to individuals only?

A Trade Descriptions Act
B Sale of Goods Act
C Late Payment of Commercial Debts (Interest) Act
D Consumer Credit Act

CHAPTER OVERVIEW

- A contract is a legally binding agreement enforceable in a court of law.

- For a valid contract to exist there must be agreement, value and an intention to create legal relations.

- For an agreement to exist there must be a valid offer and acceptance.

- An invitation to treat is an invitation to make an offer – advertisements, catalogues and price labels in shops are examples.

- An offer may lapse, be revoked, be rejected, be rejected by a counter-offer or accepted.

- Acceptance may be verbal or in writing.

- The acceptance must be unqualified – if a qualification or additional term is introduced then this is deemed to be a counter-offer and the original offer is therefore rejected.

- A valid agreement must also be supported by consideration – the consideration must be sufficient but it need not be adequate – the consideration must not be past.

- For an agreement to be enforceable in law there must have been an intention to create legal relations when the contract was made – normally in business agreements there is a presumed intention to create legal relations.

- If any terms of a contract are not fulfilled then the injured party can sue for damages for breach of contract.

- An agreement between a seller and a buyer of goods/services will normally be a contract and therefore if the buyer does not pay for the goods/services they will be in breach of contract and can be taken to an appropriate court for remedy – usually an action for the price.

- If the court agrees that the customer must pay the amount due, this can be done by an attachment of earnings order, a garnishee order, a warrant of execution or, in extreme cases, a bankruptcy notice or liquidation.

- If an individual customer is declared bankrupt or a corporate customer goes into liquidation or administration the unsecured creditors such as trade payables are unlikely to receive all of the amounts due but may receive some of the outstanding amount.

- The other legislation relevant to credit management are the Trade Descriptions Act, the Unfair Contract Terms Act, the Sale of Goods Act, the Late Payment of Commercial Debts (Interest) Act and the Consumer Credit Act.

- The Data Protection Act 1998 was introduced to ensure that there were certain restrictions about the use of data regarding individuals.

Keywords

Contract – a legally binding agreement enforceable in a court of law

Breach of contract – if one party does not carry out the terms of the contract then that party is in breach of contract

Offer – an expression of willingness to contract on a specific set of terms, which may be verbal or in writing

Offeror – the person making an offer in the hope of an acceptance

Offeree – the person to whom the offer has been made

Invitation to treat – an invitation to another party to make an offer

Revocation of an offer – an offer is revoked if the offeror removes the offer before it is accepted

Counter-offer – if an acceptance is made by an offeree which contains a new term or condition then this is deemed to be a counter-offer which is a rejection of the original offer and constitutes a new offer which, in turn, must be accepted by the original offeror for a contract to be made

Acceptance – the offeree accepts the offer

Consideration – something given, promised or done in exchange for the action of the other party

Void contract – not a contract at all and the parties are not bound by it

Voidable contract – a contract which one party may set aside

Unenforceable contract – a valid contract but if either party refuses to perform or to complete their part of the performance of the contract, the other party cannot compel them to do so

Terms – items in the contract that must be carried out to avoid breach of contract occurring

Express terms – terms that are specifically stated in the contract

Conditions – terms that are fundamental to the contract

Warranties – less important terms in the contract

Implied terms – terms of a contract that are not specifically stated but are implied by trade custom or law

Bankruptcy – an individual cannot pay their debts

Insolvency – a company cannot pay their debts

Liquidation – termination of a business operation by using its assets to discharge its liabilities

Administration – a court appointed administrator takes over the running of the company to try and return the company to solvency

Statutory demand – final demand for payment which must be issued before a petition for bankruptcy can be made

Statement of affairs – a statement of the bankrupt's assets and liabilities

Retention of title clause – states that the buyer does not obtain ownership of the goods unless and until payment is made.

Data Protection Act – law designed to make certain restrictions about the use of data about individuals and the use of personal data

Personal information – information held about an individual

Data subject – an individual who is the subject of personal data

Data controller – a person who determines the manner in which any personal data is to be processed

TEST YOUR LEARNING

Test 1

What are the three main elements that must exist for a contract to be valid?

A Offer, acceptance and value
B Offer, acceptance and valid terms
C Agreement, acceptance and value
D Agreement, value and intention to create legal relations

Test 2

Alan sees an advertisement in the local newspaper for a car costing £3,000. He answers the advert saying that he would like to buy the car but is told by the seller that there was a printing error and the advertisement should have read £5,000.

Can Alan insist on buying the car at £3,000? Explain the reason for your answer.

Test 3

A business sends out a purchase quotation to a customer for goods at a cost of £15,000. The customer replies that he would like to accept the quotation but requires that the goods are delivered the next day.

Does the business have to provide the goods at this price of £15,000?

Explain the reasons for your answer.

Test 4

What is a condition in a contract?

A A fundamental term of a contract
B A term expressly stated in the contract
C A term not expressly stated in the contract
D A term in the contract which is of lesser importance

Test 5

One of the legal remedies available for a breach of contract is "*Quantum meruit*".

What type of remedy is this?

A Compensation for loss
B Payment for part of the contract performed
C Recovery of agreed price
D Refusal to carry on with the contract

Test 6

What is a garnishee order?

A   Amount owing paid by customer's employer
B   Seizure of assets
C   Payment by a third party
D   Regular payments to the court

Test 7

What are the consequences of a bankruptcy order against an individual?

Test 8

Consider the following statements:

(i)   The Data Protection Act applies only to computer based systems.
(ii) The Data Protection Act applies to individuals and companies.

Which statements are correct?

A   (i) only
B   (ii) only
C   Both statements
D   Neither statement

Test 9

What are the eight principles of good practice of the Data Protection Act regarding the handling of personal information?

chapter 4:
METHODS OF CREDIT CONTROL

── **chapter coverage** 📖 ──

In this chapter we examine a range of techniques and methods for credit control which could be used in an organisation.

The topics covered are:

✍ Settlement discounts

✍ Methods of debt collection

SETTLEMENT DISCOUNTS

When offering to trade with a customer on credit terms, a credit limit must be set and the terms of payment communicated to the customer. These terms, such as net 30 days, must be clearly stated to the customer in writing and be on all invoices, statements etc sent to the customer.

One of the terms of trading on credit that can be offered to a customer is that of a SETTLEMENT DISCOUNT. A settlement or cash discount is an incentive to the customer to pay their outstanding invoices earlier. A percentage discount off the invoice total is offered if the customer pays within a certain period, which is shorter than the stated, normal credit terms.

Benefits of a settlement discount

The benefit to a business of offering a settlement discount to credit customers is that, if the customers take up the discount, the money will be received earlier. This means that it can be either invested to earn interest or can be used to reduce any overdraft balance thereby reducing the amount of interest paid.

Costs of a settlement discount

The cost of a settlement discount is the discount deducted from the face value of the invoice. This results in less money being received by the business although, of course, it is received sooner.

It is possible to approximate the ANNUAL COST OF OFFERING A SETTLEMENT DISCOUNT to customers by using the following formula:

$$\frac{d}{100-d} \times \frac{365}{N-D} \times 100\%$$

where d = Discount percentage given

N = Normal payment term

D = Discount payment term

HOW IT WORKS

The fuel division of SC Fuel and Glass is considering offering a settlement discount of 2% for payment within 14 days, whereas the average credit terms are payment within 60 days.

The annual cost of the discount can be estimated:

Annual cost

$$\frac{2}{100-2} \times \frac{365}{60-14} \times 100\% = 16\%$$

As it would cost 16% per annum to offer this discount it would most probably be cheaper to borrow from the bank to raise any funds required, at a rate of say 5% or 6%.

Task 1

A business currently trades on 30-day credit terms but is considering offering a settlement discount of 1% for payment within ten days of the invoice date.

What is the annual cost of this settlement discount?

A   18.4%

B   184.3%

C   1.8%

D   1.0%

Increasing credit terms

The granting of a cash discount has a positive effect on the cash flow of the business if the discount is taken up by customers.

Increasing credit terms for a customer has the opposite effect. If an increase in credit terms for a customer were agreed, for example, increasing their credit period from 30 days to 45 days, this would decrease the cash flow to the business as money from this customer would be coming into the business later.

Task 2

A business with a turnover of £2.4million currently trades on 1 month credit terms but is considering offering customers an additional month of credit.

What is the new value of receivables (debtors) balance and the annual cost of financing such a policy if the company pays interest on its overdraft at 10% per annum?

	New receivables £'000	Annual finance cost £'000
A	200	20
B	200	40
C	400	20
D	400	40

METHODS OF DEBT COLLECTION

As we have seen in the previous chapters, with good credit control procedures in place, monies will be received from credit customers. This may sometimes require encouragement such as reminder letters or telephone calls (see Chapter 5 of this Text) but payment should eventually be received. However there will be some cases in which either the debt is never collected and has to be written-off as a bad debt or the business has to resort to legal procedures to obtain payment (as seen in Chapter 3 of this Text).

Before we consider these matters, there are other methods that a business can use to minimise the possibility of either the loss of the debt or resorting to legal procedures. There are a variety of different methods of collecting the debts that are due and there are costs and benefits of each of these. They include:

- Debt collection agencies
- Factoring
- Invoice discounting
- Debt insurance

Debt collection agencies

DEBT COLLECTION AGENCIES or CREDIT COLLECTION AGENCIES are commercial organisations that specialise in the collection of debts. Most collection agencies are paid by results and charge a percentage of the debts collected for the business although some require an advance subscription for their services.

The collection agency will use appropriate methods for collecting the debts and these may include:

- Collection by telephone and letter
- Collection by personal visits
- Negotiation of a payment plan with the customer

Collection agencies are an effective method of collecting debts that are proving difficult to obtain in the normal course of trading. As collection agencies tend to be viewed as a normal business service they are unlikely to have an adverse impact on the relationship between the business and its customer. However, the collection agency does, of course, charge a fee for its services.

Factoring services

FACTORING is a financing service provided by specialist financial institutions, often subsidiaries of major banks, whereby money can be advanced to a company on the basis of the security of their receivables (debtors). A factor normally provides three main services and a company can take advantage of some or all of these:

- Provision of finance
- Administration of the receivables ledger
- Insurance against bad debts

Provision of finance by a factor

When sales on credit are made by a business, there will be a period of time elapsing before the money for those sales is received from the business's credit customers. Many businesses may find that they require the cash sooner than the customers are prepared to pay, for example to pay suppliers or reduce an overdraft. This is particularly the case for fast growing companies.

The factor advances a certain percentage of the book value of the receivables (debtors), often about 80%, as an immediate payment. The receivables are then collected by the factor and the remaining 20%, less a fee, handed over to the business when the amounts are received by the factor.

There is obviously a charge for this service and this will tend to be in two parts:

- A service charge or commission charge
- An interest charge on amounts outstanding

One further hidden cost of factoring can be a loss of customer confidence or goodwill as they will be aware that the business has factored its receivables which may have a negative impact on future relations. Many customers will view the use of a factor as an indication that a business is in financial difficulty despite the increasing use of factoring within business.

HOW IT WORKS

Suppose that the fuel division of SC Fuel and Glass were considering the use of factor finance in order to pay its suppliers earlier to take advantage of settlement discounts offered. The book value of the fuel division's receivables (debtors) is currently £700,000. The factor has agreed to advance 80% of this amount so the fuel division receives £560,000 (80% × £700,000) immediately from the factor.

The factor will then collect the receivables on behalf of SC and will pay over the remaining £140,000 less their commission and interest charges when settlement has been made by SC's customers.

Administration of the receivables (debtors) ledger by a factor

Many factoring arrangements go further than simply providing finance on the security of the receivables and will take over the entire administration of the receivables ledger. This will tend to include the following:

- Assessment of credit status
- Sending out sales invoices
- Recording sales invoices and receipts
- Sending out statements
- Sending out reminders
- Collecting payments from credit customers

The benefit to the business is not only a cost-saving from not having to run its own receivables ledger but also the expertise of the factor in this area. A fee will, of course, be charged for this service normally based upon a percentage of revenue.

Insurance against bad debts

If a factor has total control over all aspects of credit management of the receivables (debtors) ledger then they may be prepared to offer a WITHOUT RECOURSE FACTORING ARRANGEMENT. This means that the factor has no right to claim against the business if a customer does not pay. Effectively, the factor is bearing the risk of any bad debts and, naturally, will charge a higher fee for accepting this additional risk.

In other circumstances the business will retain the risk of bad debts and this is known as WITH RECOURSE FACTORING.

Task 3

Which of the following is not a service that would be provided by a factor?

A   Insurance against bad debts

B   Administration of the receivables (debtors) ledger

C   Provision of finance

D   Seizure of goods from customers who do not pay

Advantages and disadvantages of factoring

The benefits and costs of factoring can be summarised:

Advantages	Disadvantages
Advance of cash which may not be available from other sources	Cost – commission and interest
Specialist debt administration skills of the factor	Potential loss of customer goodwill
Specialist debt collection skills of the factor	Higher costs for credit insurance
Saving on in-house receivables (debtors) ledger costs	Problems of reverting to in-house debt collection in future
Reduction in bad debts cost	
Frees up management time	

Task 4

Which of the following is a disadvantage of using factor finance?

A   Cost savings

B   Reaction of some customers

C   Advance of cash

D   Reduction in bad debts

Invoice discounting

It was noted above that one of the costs of factoring is the potential loss of customer goodwill if it is known that the business is using a factor to collect its debts. The reason for this is that some customers may infer cash flow problems from the use of a factor which may not give them confidence to continue trading with the business.

One alternative, therefore, is INVOICE DISCOUNTING which is a service related to factoring. Invoice discounting is where the debts of a business are purchased by the provider of the service at a discount to their face value. The discounter simply provides cash up-front to the business at the discounted amount rather than have any involvement in the business's receivables (debtors) ledger. Under a confidential invoice-discounting agreement the business is still responsible for collecting its own debts and the business's customers will only be aware of the arrangement if they do not pay their debt. As a result invoice discounting is often chosen by businesses who wish to retain control of their own receivables ledger.

The cost to the business is the discount at which the receivables are purchased. Invoice discounting can be used for a portion of the trade receivables only and is therefore often used for a short-term or one-off exceptional cash requirement.

Task 5

Distinguish between invoice discounting and factoring arrangements.

Debt insurance

DEBT INSURANCE is insurance cover taken out against the incurring of bad debts. It has nothing to do with advances of money or collection of receivables (debtors) (as with factoring) but is simply an insurance policy to cover debts which go bad and are never settled by the customer. Such insurance, also known as credit insurance, is available from a number of sources and there are several types of policy available.

Types of debt insurance policy

The most common policy is a WHOLE TURNOVER POLICY. This type of policy can operate in one of two ways:

- The entire receivables (debtors) ledger can be covered but the amount paid out for any bad debt claim would only be normally about 80% of the claim.
- Alternatively, approximately 80% of the receivables can be insured for their entire amount and any claim on these receivables would be paid in full.

Either way under this type of policy only a proportion of bad debts will be covered for loss.

A further type of policy is an ANNUAL AGGREGATE EXCESS POLICY where bad debts are insured in total above an agreed limit or excess, in a similar way to household or car insurance policies.

Finally, it is possible to purchase insurance for a specific receivable account rather than receivables in total.

The cost of insurance will differ depending upon the insurer and the type of policy but premiums tend to be 1–2% of the amounts insured.

Task 6

A business has insured its total bad debts above an agreed limit of £2,500.

What type of insurance policy is this?

A   Partial turnover policy

B   Whole turnover policy

C   Specific receivables' (debtors') policy

D   Annual aggregate excess policy

CHAPTER OVERVIEW

- In agreeing credit terms with a customer it may be that the customer is offered a settlement discount for payment earlier than the agreed credit period – although this has a benefit to the seller in that the cash is received sooner, it also has a cost in that less is received due to the discount.

- If amounts due from credit customers cannot be recovered in the normal course of business there are a variety of other alternatives.

- A debt collection agency will use appropriate methods for collecting receivables (debtors) on a business's behalf without normally affecting customer goodwill – a fee will be charged for the agency's services.

- A factoring agreement can be for the provision of finance, the administration of the receivables (debtors) ledger and may include a without recourse agreement for protection against bad debts.

- The fees charged by a factor will depend upon the level of service provided but it can also affect customer goodwill – the benefits of factoring include an advance of cash, specialist services of the factor and a reduction in the receivables (debtors) ledger and management time and costs.

- Invoice discounting is similar to factoring although as it is anonymous will not tend to affect customer goodwill and can be used for a portion of trade receivables (debtors).

- Debt insurance is not a method of collecting receivables (debtors) but of insuring against the risk of bad debts.

Keywords

Settlement (or cash) discount – discount offered to customers for payment of the due amount earlier than the normal credit terms

Annual cost of offering settlement discount – $\dfrac{d}{100-d} \times \dfrac{365}{N-D} \times 100\%$

Debt/Credit collection agencies – commercial organisations that specialise in the collection of receivables (debtors)

Factoring – a service whereby a factor advances money on the security of a business's receivables (debtors) and may also provide other services such as administration of the receivables ledger

Without recourse factoring – a factoring arrangement where the factor bears all the risk of bad debts

With recourse factoring – a factoring arrangement where the business retains the risk of bad debts

Invoice discounting – a service whereby sales invoices are purchased for cash immediately at a discount to their face value

Debt insurance – insurance cover for bad debts either for the majority of the receivables (debtors) ledger or for specific receivables ledger accounts

Whole turnover policy – insurance for the whole receivables (debtors) ledger for say 80% of bad debts or for 80% of the receivables ledger for all bad debts

Annual aggregate excess policy – bad debts are insured for an amount above an agreed limit or excess

TEST YOUR LEARNING

Test 1

Your company currently has an average credit period of 45 days but is considering offering a 2% settlement discount for payment within ten days.

What is the approximate annual cost of this discount?

A   2.0%
B   2.13%
C   21.3%
D   213.0%

Test 2

Factoring arrangements may be either without recourse factoring or with recourse factoring.

Which of the following correctly describes one of these methods.

A   Without recourse factoring does not cover bad debts and is more expensive.

B   With recourse factoring does cover bad debts and is more expensive.

C   Without recourse factoring does cover bad debts and is more expensive.

D   With recourse factoring does not cover bad debts and is more expensive.

Test 3

Which of the following is not a cost of using a factoring service for receivables (debtors) ledger administration and collection of debts?

A   Advance of cash
B   Commission charges
C   Loss of goodwill
D   Reverting back to in-house receivables (debtors) ledger administration

Test 4

Explain two types of debt insurance policy that a business could take out.

chapter 5:
MANAGING THE SUPPLY OF CREDIT

chapter coverage 📖

In this final chapter we consider how to manage the supply of credit and prepare information to aid the collection of outstanding amounts on a timely basis. In the first two chapters of this Text we looked at the procedures required when initially granting credit to a customer. However, once an amount and period of credit has been granted to a customer, the position must be monitored on a regular basis. In this chapter we look at methods of monitoring outstanding receivables (debtors) and ways in which to encourage the payments of those debts.

The topics covered are:

✍ Transactions with credit customers

✍ Aged receivables' (debtors') analysis

✍ Bad and doubtful debts

✍ Debt collection policy

✍ Typical credit control policy and procedure

TRANSACTIONS WITH CREDIT CUSTOMERS

Once it has been agreed with a customer that they may trade on credit terms with the business, an account will be set up for that customer in the receivables (debtors) ledger. The entries in this account will be invoices and credit notes sent to the customer and receipts received from the customer.

One of the roles of the credit control team will be to monitor the transactions on each receivables's account and, in particular, the balance on the account on a regular basis.

Placing an order

The first step in the monitoring of a credit customer's activities is at the initial stage of each transaction when the customer places an order for more goods. When the initial agreement was made with the customer to trade on credit terms a CREDIT LIMIT will have been set by the credit controller for that customer.

The credit limit is the maximum amount that should be outstanding on the customer's account in the receivables (debtors) ledger at any point in time. The credit limit that is set is not an arbitrary amount; it will have been considered in the light of the credit risk of the customer and it is therefore important that the credit limit is adhered to.

When a customer places an order, the first step is to check that the value of the order does not take the customer's account over their credit limit. If the value of the order does mean that the customer's balance exceeds the credit limit then this must be discussed with the customer. Although the business will not wish to lose the sale it is important that the credit limit is not exceeded. Discussions with the customer will be required to explain that the new order can only be processed once money has been received for earlier invoices thereby leaving the account balance, including the new order value, below the credit limit.

HOW IT WORKS

One of SC Fuel and Glass's customers is Nerrington Engineering. On 14 July 20X8 the balance on their account in the receivables(debtors) ledger is £4,484.04, which is made up as shown in the table below:

		£
26/04/X8	Invoice 203741	1,350.67
28/05/X8	Invoice 203882	994.60
06/06/X8	Credit note 016452	(103.25)
14/06/X8	Invoice 203903	1,226.57
28/06/X8	Invoice 203911	1,015.45
		4,484.04

On this date Nerrington placed an order for an additional £1,245.60 of fuel, however, this will take their account balance over their credit limit of £5,000. Tom Hunt, the credit controller for the fuel division, therefore makes a telephone call to the accountant at Nerrington to explain the situation. It is agreed that Nerrington will draw a cheque for £2,242.02 which will pay off invoices 203741 and 203882 less the credit note 016452. Once this cheque has been received it is agreed that the new order will be processed and the fuel delivered.

Task 1

Why is it important that the credit limit set for a customer should not be exceeded?

If a customer's credit limit is exceeded this will have the effect of:

A   Increasing goodwill with the customer

B   Ensuring the cancellation of any settlement discount offered

C   Loss of a sale

D   Increasing the risk of non-payment of the amount due

Review of customer accounts

As well as checking that each order does not mean that the customer's balance exceeds their credit limit, each customer's account should be monitored on a regular basis. This review should involve looking for debts that are not being paid within the stated credit terms and old debts that have not been paid at all.

Accuracy of customer accounts

In order for this review of customer accounts to be meaningful, it is important that the customer accounts are kept up-to-date and accurate. This means that invoices and credit notes must be processed and posted promptly to the customer's account and that receipts of monies must also be accurately and promptly recorded in the customer's account, so that the correct balance and position can be seen at any point in time.

AGED RECEIVABLES' (DEBTORS') ANALYSIS

One particularly useful method of reviewing customer account balances is by producing an AGED RECEIVABLES' (DEBTORS') ANALYSIS. This can either be done manually or more commonly nowadays by computer.

An aged receivables' analysis splits the total balance on a customer's account into amounts which have been outstanding for particular periods of time, for example:

- Current – up to 30 days
- 31 to 60 days
- 61 to 90 days
- Over 90 days

HOW IT WORKS

We will return to the account of Nerrington Engineering in the receivables (debtors) ledger of SC Fuel and Glass. At 30 June 20X8 the account balance is made up as follows:

		£
26/04/X8	Invoice 203741	1,350.67
28/05/X8	Invoice 203882	994.60
06/06/X8	Credit note 016452	(103.25)
14/06/X8	Invoice 203903	1,226.57
28/06/X8	Invoice 203911	1,015.45
		4,484.04

The precise age of each of the outstanding invoices can be shown more clearly if an aged receivables' analysis is prepared.

Aged receivables' analysis – 30 June 20X8

	Total	Credit limit	Current <30 days	31–60 days	61–90 days	> 90 days
	£	£	£	£	£	£
Nerrington Engineering	4,484.04	5,000	2,138.77	994.60	1,350.67	–

Note that the 'current' portion is made up of Invoices 203903 and 203911 less the credit note 016452 which were all issued in June.

Task 2

You are working in the credit control department of Bourne Ltd. An extract from the company's aged receivables' (debtors') analysis at 30 September 20X4, together with information on the transactions that took place during October is shown below.

Bourne Ltd Aged Receivables' Analysis – 30 September 20X4. Credit terms: 30 days.

Customer name and ref	Total amount	Current (< 1 month)	O/s 1-2 months	O/s 2-3 months	O/s >3 months
Overton	£14,000	£5,000 B96		£9,000 B99	
Longparish	£7,000	£7,000 B95			
Stockbridge	£6,000			£3,000 B23	£3,000 B11
Andover	£15,000		£11,000 B72	£4,000 B42	
Greatley	£5,500				£5,500 B34
TOTAL	**£47,500**	**£12,000**	**£11,000**	**£16,000**	**£8,500**

Customer	Information for October X4
Overton	Paid invoice B49 £9,000. Invoice B 96 remains unpaid. Invoice B 101 £5,000 issued.
Longparish	Paid invoice B95 £7,000 Invoice B111 £6,600 issued.
Stockbridge	Paid invoice B11 £3,000. Invoice B23 remains unpaid. Invoice B102 £2,775 issued.
Andover	Paid invoice B42 £4,000. Invoice B72 £11,000 remains unpaid.
Greatley	Paid half invoice B34, balance remains unpaid.

Prepare an aged receivables' analysis as at 31 October 20X4.

Using the aged receivables' (debtors') analysis

The regular review of the aged receivables' analysis should highlight the following potential problems:

- Credit limit exceeded
- Slow payers
- Recent debts cleared but older outstanding amounts
- Old amounts outstanding but no current trading

Credit limit exceeded

As we have already seen, when an order is placed by a credit customer the first step is to check whether the customer's credit limit will be exceeded as a result. However this check may not always take place or, if the order is placed when the customer's account is not up-to-date, it may appear as if the credit limit will not be exceeded and therefore the sale is agreed.

If review of the aged receivables' analysis indicates that a customer's credit limit has been exceeded then this must be investigated.

If a customer is highlighted in the aged receivables' analysis as having exceeded their credit limit then normally the customer will be told that no further sales will be made to them until at least some of the outstanding balances have been paid. In some circumstances liaison between the receivables ledger and the sales department may result in an increase in the customer's credit limit – if they have a good payment record and are simply increasing their trade, rather than just delaying paying the amounts due. The types of checks that would be carried out before an increase in an existing customer's credit limit are similar to those carried out for a new credit customer as considered earlier in this Text.

Task 3

If an invoice to a customer was not promptly recorded in the customer's receivables (debtors) ledger account what effect might there be on the customer's account?

A   The balance may be too high.

B   The customer's credit limit may be exceeded.

C   Settlement discounts may be lost.

D   Further sales to the customer may be stopped.

Slow payers

Some businesses can be identified from the aged debtors' listing as being slow payers as they always have amounts outstanding for say 31 – 60 days and 61 – 90 days as well as current amounts. If the credit terms are 30 days from the invoice date then all amounts other than current amounts will be overdue.

In these cases consideration should be given to methods of encouraging the customer to pay earlier. This could be in the form of a reminder letter or telephone call (see later in the chapter) or perhaps the offer of a settlement discount for earlier payment (see Chapter 4 of this Text).

Recent debts cleared but older amount outstanding

If a customer is generally a regular payer and fairly recent debts have been cleared but there is still an outstanding older amount then this will normally indicate either a query over the amount outstanding or a problem with the recording of invoices, credit notes or payments received.

If there appears to be no communication from the customer about a queried invoice that would account for the old outstanding debt, then the invoice postings, credit note postings and payments received from that customer should be checked to ensure that there have been no errors which have resulted in the recording of this outstanding amount. If there appear to be no errors then the customer should be contacted in order to find out what the problem is concerning payment of this particular amount.

Old amounts outstanding and no current trading

This situation would be of some concern for the credit control team. It would appear that the customer is no longer buying from the business but still owes money from previous purchases. In this case the customer should be contacted immediately and payment sought. If no contact can be made with the customer or there is a genuine problem with payment, such as bankruptcy or liquidation, consideration should be given to writing-off the debt as bad (see later in the chapter).

HOW IT WORKS

Given below is an extract from the aged receivables' (debtors') analysis of the fuel division of SC Fuel and Glass at 30 June 20X8.

Aged receivables' analysis – 30 June 20X8

	Total	Credit limit	Current <30 days	31–60 days	61–90 days	> 90 days
	£	£	£	£	£	£
Pentagon Ltd	7,357.68	10,000	4,268.79	3,088.89		
White & Co	1,363.56	2,000	1,135.46		228.10	
Nantwich Ltd	3,745.24	5,000	732.34	1,983.36	1,029.54	
Bella Partners	4,836.47	4,000	2,295.36	2,541.11		
Manfred Paul	832.56	1,000				832.56

The position of each customer must be considered and any necessary action taken.

Pentagon Ltd   When the credit agreement with Pentagon Ltd is checked it is noted that this long standing customer is allowed 60 days of credit from the invoice date therefore there are no amounts overdue.

White & Co   The credit terms for this business are 30 days from the invoice date therefore the amount over 60 days of £228.10 is certainly overdue. However with no other overdue amounts this might indicate that there is a query regarding this figure and the customer's correspondence file should be checked. If there appears to be no queried amount then there might have been an error in the posting to the account which must also be checked.

Nantwich Ltd   The credit terms for this business are 30 days from the invoice date therefore the vast majority of the debt is outstanding. This company appears to be a slow payer and consideration should be given to encouraging them to pay within the stated credit period.

Bella Partners   Credit terms of 30 days therefore over half the debt is overdue. The customer has also exceeded their credit limit and the reason for this should be investigated. It may be decided to stop any further supplies to the customer until the overdue amounts are paid.

Manfred Paul   This is of great concern as there has been no current trading but there is an old amount outstanding. The customer should be contacted immediately with a view to collection of the amount due.

The 80/20 rule

The 80/20 rule is that in general 80% of the value of amounts owed by customers will be represented by 20% of the customer accounts. How does this affect our analysis of amounts owing?

In many cases, with large numbers of receivables (debtors) account balances, it will not be possible to analyse every single balance on a regular basis. However according to the 80/20 rule if the largest accounts making up 20% of customers are reviewed regularly this should mean that 80% of the total of receivables balances are regularly reviewed.

The remaining smaller balances making up only 20% of the receivables total can then be reviewed on a less regular basis.

Materiality

Another approach when analysing receivables is to prioritise the receivables (debtors) ledger by taking into account the materiality or significance of the debt. Thus overdue debts below a certain amount should be ignored until larger, more significant debts have been pursued as a priority.

This approach allows specific areas to be targeted by the credit control function of a business to minimise losses due to bad debts or to improve cash flow. It also takes into account that some debts may not be worth pursuing to the final degree because the time and costs involved in doing so outweigh the likely benefits.

HOW IT WORKS

A business may decide that to improve cash flow it is going to concentrate on chasing all debts over £10,000 which are up to 30 days overdue, since these are likely to be the easiest to collect, before moving on to the older but still sizeable debts.

Aged debt analysis according to materiality:

	Amount overdue	Limit
Priority 1	0 – 30 Days	Over £10,000.00
Priority 2	31 – 90 Days	Over £10,000.00
Priority 3	0 – 30 Days	Under £10,000.00
Priority 4	31 – 90 Days	Under £10,000.00
Priority 5	91+ Days	All

Care must be taken with this approach as materiality may not always just relate to monetary amount. For example:

- If a customer who has always paid on time fails to pay its latest, but relatively small debt, this could be an early warning sign that the customer is experiencing cash flow difficulties.

- Failure of a large number of small customers to pay on time, despite being each individually of relatively low significance, may indicate that there has been a problem with the despatch of invoices.

- If the amount of debts that are more than 60 days overdue is increasing, even though the individual debts are relatively small, this would warrant investigation.

Measuring the average period of credit

A business will have its own credit control policies and will set credit terms for each of its credit customers. However it is business reality that not all, and possibly not very many, customers will stick to their credit terms. Consequently, it is useful for a business to be able to determine the average period of credit taken by its customers in total. If these figures are compared over time then any improvement or deterioration of credit control procedures can be identified.

The most common method of measuring the average period of credit is using the receivables' (debtors') turnover period (see Chapter 2 of this Text). This can be compared over time and also can be compared with the payables' (creditors') turnover period. If the receivables' turnover period is consistently shorter than the payables' turnover period then this will help with liquidity.

Increase in credit limit

There will be occasions when a customer specifically requests an increase in credit limit. It may be that the customer wishes to place an order which will exceed the credit limit. The aged receivables' (debtors') listing can be a useful tool in making a decision about any increase in credit limit as it allows the credit controller to see the trading history of the customer and whether or not they have kept within their current limit in the past and paid according to their credit terms.

Task 4

The aged receivables' (debtors') analysis for a business shows that a customer has £736.50 owing from the current period and £104.00 due from the 61 – 90 day period.

What course of action should be taken concerning this customer?

BAD AND DOUBTFUL DEBTS

The aged receivables' (debtors') analysis can also be used to identify debts which might be BAD DEBTS or DOUBTFUL DEBTS.

A bad debt is one where it is almost certain that the monies will not be received. A doubtful debt is one where there is some doubt over the eventual receipt of the money but it is not such a clear case as a bad debt. The reason for the distinction between the two is that in the financial accounting records a bad debt is written-off and no longer appears in the ledger or on the statement of financial position (balance sheet) whereas a doubtful debt has an allowance (provision) made against it, so it still appears in the ledger, and on the statement of financial position where it is netted-off against the receivables balance.

Identification of bad and doubtful debts

As the people dealing with the customer accounts and analysing the aged receivables (debtors), the credit control team are in a position to be able to assess potential bad debts. They should ensure that when doing so they use all available information. This may include the following:

- Evidence of long outstanding debts from the aged receivables' analysis
- A one-off outstanding debt when more recent debts have been cleared
- Correspondence with customers
- Outstanding older debts and no current business with the customer
- A sudden or unexpected change in payment patterns

- Request for an extension of credit terms
- Press comment
- Information from the sales team

When considering the aged receivables' analysis, earlier in this chapter, we saw that the pattern of the ageing of receivables for individual customers can give a clue as to any problems with each individual customer. Such potential problems must be investigated and the outcome may be that a bad or doubtful debt is identified.

HOW IT WORKS

Given again is the extract from the fuel division's aged receivables' (debtors') analysis at 30 June 20X8.

Aged receivables' analysis – 30 June 20X8

	Total	Credit limit	Current <30 days	31–60 days	61–90 days	> 90 days
	£	£	£	£	£	£
Pentagon Ltd	7,357.68	10,000	4,268.79	3,088.89		
White & Co	1,363.56	2,000	1,135.46		228.10	
Nantwich Ltd	3,745.24	5,000	732.34	1,983.36	1,029.54	
Bella Partners	4,836.47	4,000	2,295.36	2,541.11		
Manfred Paul	832.56	1,000				832.56

The two debts which may be under consideration are the old debts owing by White & Co and by Manfred Paul.

Upon investigation it is discovered that the amount of £228.10 is in dispute with White & Co as they have no record of having received this delivery of fuel. SC's despatch team are still trying to find evidence that the fuel was supplied but, as yet, they can find no delivery note to support the invoice that was sent out. This could be viewed as a doubtful debt as there is certainly some doubt as to whether this was in fact a valid sale or not.

Manfred Paul is an individual customer with whom SC has traded periodically. Upon contacting Manfred Paul it has been discovered that he has been declared bankrupt and has no funds to pay his suppliers. This debt will probably be declared a bad debt.

Information about potential bad and doubtful debts

If a member of the credit control team discovers that a debt is highly likely to be classified as bad or doubtful then it will probably not be that person's responsibility to write the debt off or provide against it. This is normally the role of a more senior member of the accounting function. Therefore it is important that all information about potential bad or doubtful debts is clearly communicated to the relevant person within the accounting function as this will have an impact on the preparation of the financial statements for the business.

Task 5

Which of the following is correct about bad and doubtful debts?

A   A bad debt will not be received and an allowance (provision) is made.

B   A doubtful debt may be received but it is written off.

C   A bad debt may be received and an allowance (provision) is made.

D   A doubtful debt may not be received and an allowance (provision) is made.

DEBT COLLECTION POLICY

As we have seen when credit is extended to a customer the credit terms will be made clear. However, many customers will not adhere to those credit terms and will effectively make use of what they might view as free credit by taking as long as possible to pay what is due.

Accordingly, most businesses will have some sort of policy regarding the collection of debts and the processes that will take place to chase up any outstanding amounts.

Debt collection process

The debt collection process starts with the sending out of the sales invoice on which the credit terms should be clearly stated. Thereafter, a variety of reminders are sent to the customer to encourage them to pay within the credit terms and, for those overdue debts, a further series of reminders.

A typical debt collection process can be illustrated:

Invoice sent
|
Statement sent
|
Telephone reminder
|
Reminder letters
|
Stop list
|
External means of
debt collection

(dealt with in Chapter 4 of this Text)

Sales invoice

Once a sale has been made, the first communication with the customer is to send out the sales invoice. This should be promptly sent, as soon as the goods or services have been provided, and should clearly state the payment period agreed.

Statements

Most businesses will then send a monthly STATEMENT to the customer showing the balance at the end of that month and how that is made up, ie invoices, credit notes, payments received. The statement may include a remittance advice which is to encourage the customer to pay the amounts due and also indicates which invoices are covered by this payment.

Telephone calls

An OVERDUE DEBT is one which has not been paid within the stated credit period. Once a debt has become overdue it is common practice to telephone the customer to enquire about the situation, determine whether or not there is a query over the amount due and agree when the debt will be paid.

When making this type of telephone call particular attention should be given to the following matters:

- Discussion with the customer should always be courteous.

- The precise amount of the debt should be pointed out and the fact that it is overdue.

- It should be established whether there is any query with regard to the debt, and if so, any appropriate action agreed to resolve the query.

- If there is no query then a date for payment of the debt should be established.

It is important to keep precise notes of what has been agreed in a telephone conversation with a customer as this may need to be confirmed by letter. For example, if a customer agrees over the telephone to clear an outstanding amount by paying in four instalments then this should be confirmed to the customer in writing.

Reminder letters

If there has been no response to telephone calls requesting payment of the overdue amount then this is followed up with a REMINDER LETTER.

This first reminder letter is designed to point out the facts – the amount outstanding – and as a reminder or encouragement to pay the amount due. As with all letters to customers it must be courteous and succinct as well as firm.

The reminder letter will be sent out when the debts are a certain amount of time overdue. The time-scale of the reminder letter will depend upon the organisation's policy towards debt collection but usually is sent out seven days after a debt becomes overdue. Accordingly, if an invoice is sent to a customer with 30-day credit terms then the first reminder letter will be sent out 37 days after the invoice.

The first reminder letter will normally be sent to the person with day-to-day responsibility for payment of suppliers.

An example of a typical first reminder letter is given below:

Date

Dear Sir

Account No: 385635/A

I do not appear to have received payment of the invoices detailed below. I trust that this is an oversight and that you will arrange for immediate payment to be made. If you are withholding payment for any reason, please contact me urgently and I will be pleased to assist you.

Invoice No	Terms	Due date	Amount
			£

If you have already made payment please advise me and accept my apology for having troubled you.

Yours faithfully
Credit controller

Practice in this area will vary between organisations and some organisations will send out an initial reminder letter before a telephone call is made to the customer.

Final reminder letter

If there is no response from the initial reminder letter then there will be little point in sending a second reminder letter. However, at this stage a telephone call might be useful to clear up any misunderstanding and to assess whether further action is required.

The options for the business at this point are generally:

- To put the debt into the hands of a debt collection agency (see Chapter 4 of this Text)

- To take the customer to court for payment (see Chapter 3 of this Text)

- To suspend any further sales to the customer by placing the customer on a STOP LIST until payment is received

Whatever measures are to be taken, a final reminder letter must be sent to the customer detailing this action if payment is not received. This final reminder letter is normally sent to a senior member of the management team such as the chief accountant or finance director.

Typical letters are shown below.

Debt collection letter

Date

Dear Sir

Account No: 385635/A

Further to our invoices detailed below and the reminder letter dated 14 July 20X8 I do not appear to have received payment. If you are withholding payment for any reason, please contact me urgently and I will be pleased to assist you.

Invoice No	Terms	Due date	Amount
			£

I regret that unless payment is received within the next seven days I will have no alternative but to put the collection of the amounts due into the hands of a third party.

If you have already made the payment please advise me and accept my apology for having troubled you.

Yours faithfully
Credit controller

Court proceedings letter

Date

Dear Sir

Account No: 385635/A
Total amount outstanding £1,138.30

Despite the previous reminders and telephone calls we have still not received your payment in settlement of the above account total. You have promised payment on a number of occasions but no payment has been received to date.

We regret that due to the above we have no alternative but to consider the Small Claims procedure in the County Court in order to recover the sum outstanding. Prior to us taking such action we would, however, wish to give you one final opportunity to make payment. We will therefore delay submission of the claim to the County Court for a period of seven days from the date of this letter in the hope that the account is settled. We will not enter into any further correspondence regarding this matter other than through the County Court.

Please note that if we are forced to take legal action you may become liable for the costs of such action which, if successful, may affect your future credit rating.

Yours faithfully
Credit controller

Stop list letter

> Date
>
> Dear Sir
>
> **Account No: 385635/A**
>
> Further to our invoices detailed below, I do not appear to have received payment. I trust that this is an oversight and that you will arrange for immediate payment to be made. If you are withholding payment for any reason, please contact me urgently and I will be pleased to assist you.
>
> | Invoice No | Terms | Due date | Amount £ |
> |------------|-------|----------|----------|
>
> I regret that unless payment is received within the next seven days I will have no alternative but to stop any further sales on credit to you until the amount owing is cleared in full. If you have already made payment please advise me and accept my apology for having troubled you. Please note that if we are forced to take legal action you may become liable for the costs of such action which, if successful, may affect your future credit rating.
>
> Yours faithfully
> Credit controller

HOW IT WORKS

The glass division of SC Fuel and Glass has the following written policy for debt collection.

Debt collection policy

1. Invoices should be sent out on the same day as goods are delivered.

2. An aged analysis of receivables (debtors) should be produced monthly.

3. Statements are sent to credit customers on the first working day of each month.

4. A reminder letter is sent when a debt is seven days overdue.

5. A telephone call to chase payment must be made when a debt is 14 days overdue.

6. When the debt is 30 days overdue the customer will be placed on the stop list and a letter sent confirming this. A meeting should then be arranged with the customer in order to discuss the account position.

7. When the debt is 60 days overdue it will be placed in the hands of a debt collection agency or legal proceedings will be commenced based upon the decision of the financial controller.

An invoice was sent to Yarrow Ltd, for £8,570 on 1 June on 30-day credit terms. This debt is still outstanding at 30 June. The process that would follow, providing that the money was not received, would be:

- 7 July – first reminder letter sent

- 14 July – telephone reminder

- 30 July – placed on stop list and final reminder letter sent. Meeting arranged to resolve the payment problem.

- 29 August – decision taken regarding final treatment of overdue amount

Task 6

What factors are important when planning to make a telephone call to a customer regarding an overdue amount?

TYPICAL CREDIT CONTROL POLICY AND PROCEDURE

Finally, to complete this chapter we reproduce here a typical credit control policy and procedure as published in the AAT draft delivery guidance for this Unit.

New accounts

1   One bank reference and two trade references are required.

2   A credit reference agency report and the last three years' published accounts for limited companies needs to be analysed.

3   A credit reference agency report and the last three years' accounts for a sole trader need to be analysed.

Existing customers

4   A credit reference agency report to be obtained on an annual basis together with the latest annual accounts (either from Companies House or directly from the customer). Both documents to be reviewed.

5   A trading history review to be undertaken annually to review the performance against credit limits and terms of payment.

6   Annual review of usage of the customers' credit limit and to ensure that an outdated credit limit is not in existence. This is particularly important where the trade with the customer has reduced over the past year.

Credit terms

7   Standard terms are 30 days from invoice. Any extension to be authorised by the finance director.

8   A 2% settlement discount to be offered to all accounts with a profit margin of 50% or greater or with a profit margin of 30% and a value in excess of £50,000 or with the credit controller's discretion.

Debt collection process

9   Invoices to be despatched on day of issue, (day of issue to be no more than two days after date of delivery).

10   Statements to be despatched in the second week of the month.

11   Aged receivables' (debtors') analysis to be produced and reviewed on a weekly basis.

12   Reminder letter to be sent once an account is overdue.

13   Telephone chaser for accounts 15 days overdue.

14   Customer on stop list if no payment is received within five days of the telephone chaser. Computerised sales order processing system updated and automatic e-mail sent to the customer contact and the account manager (sales person).

15   Letter threatening legal action if payment not received within 30 days of the first letter.

16   Legal proceedings/debt collection agency instructed subject to approval of the finance director.

17   Prepare a report suggesting an appropriate allowance (provision) for bad or doubtful debts.

18   If at any stage in the process the customer is declared insolvent or bankrupt then contact the insolvency practitioner in order to register the debt and notify the financial accountant so that the sales tax (VAT) can be reclaimed.

The AAT delivery guidance states that "Candidates need to be able to explain the stages in the credit control policy and procedure and why the stages are important. Candidates may also be required to use a given policy in a scenario and decide upon an action which needs to be taken."

CHAPTER OVERVIEW

- One of the roles of the credit control team is to monitor the transactions and balances on credit customers' accounts.

- When an order is placed by a customer it should be checked that the value of the order will not lead to the customer exceeding their agreed credit limit.

- An aged receivables' (debtors') analysis is a useful tool in monitoring credit customers' accounts and can be used to identify credit limits exceeded, slow payers, problem amounts and potential bad and doubtful debts.

- The credit control team should be aware of factors that might indicate a possible bad debt or doubtful debt and the appropriate member of the accounting function should be immediately informed of all the circumstances if such a debt is identified.

- The debt collection process starts with the sending out of sales invoices and statements – if payment is not received within the stated credit period this will be followed by reminder letters, telephone reminders and eventually action such as cessation of trading, use of a debt collection agency or legal proceedings.

- Most businesses will have a written debt collection policy which must be followed.

Keywords

Credit limit – the maximum amount that should be outstanding on a customer's receivables (debtors) ledger account at any point in time

Aged receivables' (debtors') analysis – an analysis of each individual receivable's balance split into amounts that have been outstanding for particular periods of time

Bad debts – debts where it is almost certain that the monies due will not be received

Doubtful debts – debts where there is some doubt over whether the monies due will eventually be received

Statement – analysis of the amount due by a customer and the transactions on their account for the last period which is periodically sent to the customer

Overdue debt – a debt which has not been paid within the stated credit period

Reminder letter – a letter sent to a customer encouraging payment of an overdue debt

Stop list – a list of customers to whom goods should not be sold on credit

TEST YOUR LEARNING

Test 1

If customer accounts in the receivables (debtors) ledger are not kept accurately up-to-date then this can cause a number of problems.

Which of the following is not one of those problems?

A   Problem items may not be highlighted in the aged receivables' (debtors') listing.

B   Incorrect statements may be sent out to customers.

C   The correct goods may not be despatched to the customer.

D   Orders may be taken which exceed the customer's credit limit.

Test 2

A customer of a business has an outstanding balance on its receivables (debtors) ledger account of £17,685 at 31 July. This balance is made up as follows:

		£
22 May	Inv 093106	2,184
3 June	Inv 093182	3,785
21 June	Inv 093265	4,839
2 July	Credit note 04623	(536)
5 July	Inv 093321	3,146
20 July	Inv 093346	4,267
		17,685

The customer's name is Fording Ltd and the company has a credit limit of £20,000.

Use the table below to complete the aged receivables' analysis for this customer as at 31 July.

Customer	Total	Credit limit	Current <30 days	31–60 days	61–90 days	90 days
	£	£	£	£	£	£

Test 3

Which of the following might typically be highlighted by analysis of an aged receivables' (debtors') listing?

(i) Slow payers
(ii) Settlement discounts taken
(iii) Exceeding a credit limit
(iv) Potential bad debts
(v) Credit terms
(vi) Items in dispute

A (i), (ii), (iv) and (v)
B (iii), (iv), (v) and (vi)
C (i), (iii), (iv) and (v)
D (i), (iii), (iv) and (vi)

Test 4

Given below are extracts from an aged receivables' (debtors') analysis for a company at 30 September:

	Total	Credit limit	Current <30 days	31–60 days	61–90 days	> 90 days
	£	£	£	£	£	£
Kerry & Co	5,389	8,000	4,999		390	
Marshall Ltd	16,378	15,000	16,378			
Leyton Ltd	5,377	10,000	1,854	1,757	1,766	

Credit terms are that payment is due within 30 days of the invoice date.

For each customer state what the aged receivables' listing might indicate about that customer and what if any action might be required.

Customer	Comment and action
Kerry & Co	
Marshall Ltd	
Leyton Ltd	

Test 5

What information available to the credit control team might indicate the existence of a bad or doubtful debt?

Test 6

A company has a policy of granting credit terms of 30 days from the invoice date. Once an invoice is seven days overdue a telephone call is made to the customer to enquire about the debt. Once an invoice is 14 days overdue a reminder letter is sent to the customer. Once an invoice is 30 days overdue the customer is placed on the stop list and a letter is sent informing them of this.

Given below is an extract from the company's aged receivables (debtors) listing at 30 June.

	Total	Credit limit	Current <30 days	31–60 days	61–90 days	> 90 days
	£	£	£	£	£	£
Travis Ltd	4,678	5,000		4,678		
Muse Ltd	3,557	5,000	2,669	888		
Keane Ltd	6,248	8,000	5,145		1,103	

- The balance owing by Travis Ltd is made up of invoice number 467824 dated 15 May.

- Invoice number 467899 to Muse Ltd for £2,669 was dated 2 June and invoice number 467831 for £888 was dated 23 May.

- Invoice number 467781 for £1,103 was dated 22 April.

For each customer determine what action if any is necessary according to the credit collection policy and draft any letters that might be necessary to send to these customers.

ANSWERS TO CHAPTER TASKS

CHAPTER 1 Managing the granting of credit

1   The ordering cycle involves the following:

- Customer places an order
- Customer credit status is established
- Customer is offered credit
- Goods are despatched
- Goods are delivered
- Invoice is despatched

2   C

3   There are two main risks in granting credit to a customer:

- The customer will exceed the stated credit period therefore depriving the seller of the use of the cash.

- The customer may never pay at all – a bad debt.

4

Credit reference agency	External
Staff knowledge	Internal
Financial analysis of customer accounts	Internal
Bank reference	External
The internet	External

CHAPTER 2 Granting credit to customers

1   C

2

	%
Return on capital employed	15.6

Return on capital employed $\quad = \quad \dfrac{76,000}{488,000} \times 100$

$\qquad\qquad\qquad\qquad = \quad 15.6\%$

3

	Days
Inventory (stock) turnover	41
Receivables' (debtors') turnover	48
Payables' (creditors') turnover	47

Inventory turnover $= \dfrac{77,000}{686,000} \times 365$

$= $ 41 days

Receivables' turnover $= \dfrac{130,000}{980,000} \times 365$

$= $ 48 days

Payables' turnover $= \dfrac{89,000}{686,000} \times 365$

$= $ 47 days

4

	Workings	
Gearing ratio	100,000/(200,000 +188,000)	26%
Interest cover	(45,000+6,000)/6,000	8.5 times
EBITDA based interest cover	(45,000+6,000+12,000)/6,000	10.5 times

5   The information provided in the bank reference looks positive. It is not as good as "undoubted" but suggests that the customer is probably OK and a reasonable risk.

The trade reference also looks fairly positive in that XYZ ltd offers 45 day payment terms and receives prompt payment which gives some confidence. However the amount of credit they offer is only £5,000 whereas Conrad Ltd has applied to you for credit of £8,000.

In conjunction with perhaps another trade reference and satisfactory other internal and external information about Conrad Ltd, a decision may be taken to grant Conrad's credit request.

6   Reasons for not agreeing to trade on credit with a customer might include the following:

- A non-committal or unsatisfactory bank reference

- Poor trade references

- Concerns about the validity of any trade references submitted

- Adverse press comment about the potential customer

- Information from a member of the business's credit circle

- Poor credit agency report

- Indications of business weakness from analysis of the financial statements

- Lack of historical financial statements available due to being a recently started company

CHAPTER 3   Legislation and credit control

1   John cannot insist on purchasing the car at the lower price as the price ticket is an invitation to treat rather than an offer. John makes the offer to buy the car for £2,395 but this is rejected by the salesman.

2   D

3   A

4   Bankruptcy is where an individual is unable to pay their debts whereas insolvency is where a company is unable to pay its debts.

5   The role of an insolvency practitioner under an administration order is to try to save the company or at the very least to achieve a better result for the payables (creditors) than a liquidation.

6   D

CHAPTER 4   Methods of credit control

1   A

$$\text{Cost of discount} \quad = \quad \frac{1}{100-1} \times \frac{365}{30-10} \times 100$$

$$= \quad 18.4\%$$

2   C

Current receivables (debtors) = £2.4m/12 = £200,000

New receivables = £2.4m × 2/12 = £400,000

Additional finance required for the extra £200,000 tied up in working capital @10% = £20,000.

3   D

4   B

Some customers may view the use of a factor by a business as a sign that the business is in financial or cash flow difficulty and therefore may re-consider whether to carry on trading with them.

5   Invoice discounting is simply the provision of finance to a business by the purchase of its invoices at a discount. There is no involvement with the business's receivables (debtors) ledger. Under a factoring agreement the factor will normally run the receivables ledger and collect the debts as well as providing finance in the form of an advance based upon a percentage of the face value of the receivables.

6   D

CHAPTER 5   Managing the supply of credit

1   D

The credit limit that is set for a credit customer will have been set by the credit controller as part of his assessment of the risk of the customer. Therefore if this credit limit is exceeded it is potentially increasing the risk that the business faces from these sales on credit.

2   **Bourne Ltd   Aged receivables analysis as at 31 October 20X4**

Customer name and ref	Total amount	Current < 1 month	O/s 1-2 months	O/s 2-3 months	O/s >3 months
Overton	£10,000	£5,000 B101	£5,000 B96		
Longparish	£6,600	£6,600 B111			
Stockbridge	£5,775	£2,775 B102			£3,000 B23
Andover	£11,000			£11,000 B72	
Greatley	£2,750				£2,750 B34
TOTAL	**£36,125**	**£14,375**	**£5,000**	**£11,000**	**£5,750**

3   B

If an invoice is not promptly recorded in the customer's receivables (debtors) ledger account then this may mean that the next time that the customer places an order the balance on his account is too low. When the credit limit is checked to ensure that it is not exceeded by the new order value the sale might be authorised even though the new order may in fact take the customer over their credit limit.

4   As the customer has current amounts due but no 30-to-61 day amounts due it could be assumed that he was a regular payer and therefore that the £104 due from 61 to 90 days was an amount that was being queried. The best course of action would be to check the customer's correspondence file to determine whether this amount was being queried and also to check that the amount was, in fact, due from this customer and that there were no errors in posting to the customer's account. Then a telephone call should be made to the customer to enquire why this overdue amount has not been paid.

5   D

A bad debt is one where it is almost certain that the money is not going to be received whereas a doubtful debt is one where there is some doubt over whether the money will be received but no certainty. The importance of the distinction between a bad and a doubtful debt is in their respective accounting treatments. A bad debt is written-off from the financial statements whereas an allowance (provision) is made for a doubtful debt.

6   When making a telephone call to discuss an overdue debt with a customer the following factors are of particular importance:

- Discussion with the customer should always be courteous.

- The precise amount of the debt should be pointed out and the fact that it is overdue.

- It should be established whether there is any query with regard to the debt and, if so, any appropriate action should be agreed to resolve the query.

- If there is no query then a date for payment of the debt should be established.

- All of this should be recorded for future reference.

TEST YOUR LEARNING – ANSWERS

CHAPTER 1   Managing the granting of credit

1   D

2   D

3   Net 14 days 3% discount for payment within seven days

4   C

CHAPTER 2   Granting credit to customers

1   C

2   The information provided in the trade reference looks fairly positive in that SK Traders offer monthly payment terms which are only occasionally overrun. However the amount of credit they offer is only £8,000 whereas Caterham Ltd has applied to you for credit of £15,000.

In conjunction with perhaps another trade reference and other internal and external information about Caterham Ltd this trade reference may give you some confidence in the company.

3   Credit reference agencies can provide a variety of information about companies and individuals which may include the following:

- Historical financial statements
- Directors' details
- Payment history
- Details of any insolvency proceedings or bankruptcy orders
- Bankers' opinions
- Credit rating

4   C

5

	20X9	20X8
Gross profit margin	22.0%	21.3%
Net profit margin	12.0%	11.7%
Return on capital employed (120/1,125; 110/1,078)	10.7%	10.2%
Current ratio	0.5 to 1	0.7 to 1
Quick ratio	0.3 to 1	0.4 to 1
Payables' (creditors') payment period	75 days	79 days
Interest cover	4 times	5.5 times

6

ACORN ENTERPRISES

Finance Partner
Little Partners

Date

Dear Sir

Re: Request for credit facilities

Thank you for your enquiry regarding the provision of credit facilities to yourselves for £8,000 of credit on 60-day terms. We have taken up your bank and trade references and examined your latest set of financial statements.

Although your references are satisfactory we have some concerns about your profitability and liquidity. Clearly, your overall profitability and liquidity position have improved since 20X7 but their levels are still lower than we would normally expect in order to grant a credit facility.

However due to your bank and trade references we are happy to offer you a credit facility for six months at the end of which time the movement on your account will be reviewed and the position re-assessed. The credit limit that we can offer you would initially be £3,000 and the payment terms are strictly 30 days from the invoice date.

Thank you for your interest in our company and we look forward to trading with you on the basis set out above.

Yours faithfully

Jo Wilkie

Credit manager

7

Finance Director

Dawn Ltd
Date

Dear Sir

Re: Request for credit facilities

Thank you for your enquiry regarding the provision of credit facilities to yourselves for £5,000 of credit on 30-day terms. We have taken up your trade references and examined your latest set of financial statements.

Unfortunately we are concerned about your levels of profitability, gearing and liquidity in the most recent year and also have some concerns about one of the trade references from Johannesson Partners.

On balance, we are not in a position to grant your request for trade credit at the current time although we would, of course, be delighted to trade with you on a cash basis. If you do not wish to trade on this basis and would like to enquire about credit terms in the future then we would be delighted to examine your current year's financial statements when they are available.

Thank you for your interest shown in our business.

Yours faithfully

Credit controller

CHAPTER 3 Legislation and credit control

1   D

2   Alan cannot insist on purchasing the car for £3,000 as the advertisement is an invitation to treat not an offer. When Alan answers the advertisement he is making an offer to purchase the car for £3,000 which can be accepted or rejected by the seller.

3   The business does not have to supply the goods at £15,000 as the additional term for delivery the next day is a counter-offer which rejects the original offer.

4   A

5   B

6   C

7   The consequences of a bankruptcy order against an individual are:

- The official receiver takes control of the assets of the individual.

- A statement of the assets and liabilities is drawn up – this is known as a statement of affairs.

- The receiver summons a meeting of all those to whom money is owed within 12 weeks of the bankruptcy order.

- The creditors appoint a trustee in bankruptcy.

- The assets of the individual are realised and distribution is made to the various creditors.

8   D

The Data Protection Act applies to both paper-based systems and computer systems and protects personal information. Personal information is information held about living individuals.

9   The eight principles of good practice of the Data Protection Act are that personal information must be:

- Fairly and lawfully processed

- Processed for limited purposes

- Adequate, relevant and not excessive

- Accurate and up-to-date

- Not kept for longer than necessary

- Processed in line with the data subject's rights

- Kept securely

- Not transferred to countries outside the EU unless such data is adequately protected in those countries.

CHAPTER 4   Methods of credit control

1   C

Cost of discount $= \dfrac{2}{100-2} \times \dfrac{365}{45-10} \times 100$

$= \quad 21.3\%$

2   C

3   A – this is a benefit not a cost.

4 Any two of the following:

- A whole turnover policy is where either the whole receivables (debtors) ledger is covered but the amount paid out for any bad debt is only, say, 80% of the claim or 80% of the receivables ledger is covered for their entire amount and any claim on these would be paid in full.

- An annual aggregate excess policy is where bad debts are insured in total above an agreed limit or excess.

- A specific receivables policy is where only specific receivables ledger customers are insured for the bad debt risk.

CHAPTER 5   Managing the supply of credit

1   C   The goods will be despatched before the receivables (debtors) ledger is written up therefore despatch will not be affected.

2

Customer	Total	Credit limit	Current <30 days	31–60 days	61–90 days	90 days
	£	£	£	£	£	£
Fording Ltd	17,685	20,000	6,877	8,624	2,184	

3   D

4

Customer	Comment and action
Kerry & Co	The vast majority of this customer's debt is current with a relatively small amount outstanding in 61 to 90 days. This may indicate that there was some dispute or error about this outstanding amount which should be investigated.
Marshall Ltd	This customer has exceeded their credit limit which should be investigated. However the balance is all current and if this is a valued and reliable customer it may be considered necessary to increase their credit limit to facilitate higher levels of trading.
Leyton Ltd	This customer would appear to be a persistently late payer with approximately one-third of their total debt spread over each month for the last three months. The credit controller will need to re-affirm the credit terms of 30 days with the customer and possibly offer some incentive for earlier payment such as a settlement discount.

5   Information that might be available to the credit control team which might indicate a bad or doubtful debt includes:

- Evidence of long outstanding debts from the aged receivables' (debtors') analysis

- A one-off outstanding debt when more recent debts have been cleared

- Correspondence with receivables (debtors)

- Outstanding older debts and no current business with the customer

- A sudden or unexpected change in payment patterns

- Request for an extension of credit terms

- Press comment

- Information from the sales team

6   **Travis Ltd**

This amount is 14 days overdue and therefore a reminder letter must be sent to the customer.

| Purchase ledger manager |
| Travis Ltd |
| 30 June |
| Dear Sir |
| I do not appear to have received payment of the invoice detailed below. I trust that this is an oversight and that you will arrange for immediate payment to be made. If you are with-holding payment for any reason, please contact me urgently and I will be pleased to assist you. |

Invoice No	Terms	Due date	Amount
			£
467824	30 days	14 June	4,678.00

| If you have already made payment please advise me and accept my apology for having troubled you. |
| Yours faithfully |
| Credit Controller |

Muse Ltd

The invoice number 467831 for £888 is seven days overdue and therefore a telephone call is necessary to the purchase ledger manager explaining that the amount is overdue, determining whether there is any query with the amount and agreeing a date for payment of the overdue amount.

Keane Ltd

The invoice for £1,103 is over two months overdue and should be investigated. Furthermore the policy is that once an amount is 30 days overdue the customer is put on the stop list. It would appear that this has not happened as Keane Ltd have recent amounts (< 30 days) due totalling £5,145.

A letter would be sent to the financial controller of Keane Ltd.

Financial Controller

Keane Ltd

Date

Dear Sir

Further to our invoice detailed below, I do not appear to have received payment. I trust that this is an oversight and that you will arrange for immediate payment to be made. If you are withholding payment for any reason, please contact me urgently and I will be pleased to assist you.

Invoice No	Terms	Due date	Amount
			£
467781	30 days	22 May	1,103.00

I regret that unless payment is received within the next seven days I will have no alternative but to stop any further sales on credit to you until the amount owing is cleared in full. If you have already made payment please advise me and accept my apology for having troubled you.

Yours faithfully

Credit Controller

INDEX

Notes

REVIEW FORM

How have you used this Text?
(Tick one box only)

☐ Home study

☐ On a course_____

☐ Other _____

Why did you decide to purchase this Text? *(Tick one box only)*

☐ Have used BPP Texts in the past

☐ Recommendation by friend/colleague

☐ Recommendation by a college lecturer

☐ Saw advertising

☐ Other _____

During the past six months do you recall seeing/receiving either of the following?
(Tick as many boxes as are relevant)

☐ Our advertisement in Accounting Technician

☐ Our Publishing Catalogue

Which (if any) aspects of our advertising do you think are useful?
(Tick as many boxes as are relevant)

☐ Prices and publication dates of new editions

☐ Information on Text content

☐ Details of our free online offering

☐ None of the above

Your ratings, comments and suggestions would be appreciated on the following areas of this Text.

	Very useful	Useful	Not useful
Introductory section	☐	☐	☐
Quality of explanations	☐	☐	☐
How it works	☐	☐	☐
Chapter tasks	☐	☐	☐
Chapter Overviews	☐	☐	☐
Test your learning	☐	☐	☐
Index	☐	☐	☐

	Excellent	Good	Adequate	Poor
Overall opinion of this Text	☐	☐	☐	☐

Do you intend to continue using BPP Products?   ☐ Yes   ☐ No

Please note any further comments and suggestions/errors on the reverse of this page. The author of this edition can be e-mailed at: suedexter@bpp.com

Please return to: Sue Dexter, Publishing Director, BPP Learning Media Ltd, FREEPOST, London, W12 8BR.

REVIEW FORM (continued)

TELL US WHAT YOU THINK

Please note any further comments and suggestions/errors below.